Author

Daphne Hall is an editor for Rightsnet, and a freelance writer on welfare rights.

Acknowledgements

Many thanks are due to the authors of the previous editions: Alison Gillies, Henri Krishna, Simon Osborne, Judith Paterson, Jon Shaw, David Simmons, Angela Toal and Mark Willis. For assisting with this edition, thank you to David Simmons, Simon Osborne and Gwyneth King. Thanks are due to Nicola Johnston for her efficient and thorough editing, and for managing the production. Thanks also to Katherine Dawson for producing the index and Kathleen Armstrong for proofreading the text.

About Child Poverty Action Group

Child Poverty Action Group is a national charity working for the abolition of child poverty in the UK and for the improvement of the lives of low-income families.

To help achieve this goal, we have developed a high level of expertise in the welfare benefits system. We use this to support thousands of frontline advisers with our expert training and free helplines, enabling them to give families the best information and advice.

We also publish a widely used series of practitioner handbooks: our annual *Welfare Benefits and Tax Credits Handbook* (known as 'the adviser's bible') is used by Citizens Advice Bureaux, local authorities and law centres throughout the UK.

Our policy, campaigning and lobbying work builds support for policy improvements to help children living in poverty. We host the End Child Poverty campaign, a national coalition of charities, faith groups and other organisations working to hold the government to its target of beating child poverty by 2020.

If you would like to help with our campaign to end child poverty, please visit our website at www.cpag.org.uk. You can also get the latest news by following us on Facebook (www.facebook.com/cpaguk) and Twitter @CPAGUK.

Keeping up to date

Advisers can get the latest information on universal credit by booking on a CPAG training course. We can also provide your workplace with in-house training. See www.cpag.org.uk/training for more information.

Our *Welfare Benefits and Tax Credits Handbook* 2017/18, published in April 2017, contains the latest information on universal credit, personal independence payment and other welfare reform measures. It also tells you all you need to know about entitlement to benefits and tax credits from April 2017.

Getting advice

Your local Citizens Advice Bureau or other advice centre can give you advice and support on benefits. See www.citizensadvice.org.uk if you live in England or Wales, or www.cas.org.uk if you live in Scotland.

CPAG has an advice line for advisers and support workers.

For advisers and support workers in the UK:
Telephone: 020 7812 5231, Monday to Friday 10am to 12pm and 2pm to 4pm

Email: advice@cpag.org.uk (email advice is limited to enquiries specifically about universal credit, child benefit, child tax credit or working tax credit)

For advisers and support workers in Scotland:
Telephone: 0141 552 0552, Monday to Thursday 10am to 4pm and Friday 10am to 12pm

Email: advice@cpagscotland.org.uk

Contents

Chapter 1
Introduction

This chapter covers:

1. What is universal credit?

2. What is happening to the old benefits system?

3. How is universal credit administered?

4. How is universal credit different?

What you need to know

- Universal credit is a benefit for people of working age who are in or out of work. It has been gradually introduced throughout Great Britain since October 2013.

- Universal credit is administered by the Department for Work and Pensions and is claimed online.

- The amount of your universal credit depends on your income and savings – ie, it is 'means tested'. You do not need to have paid national insurance contributions to qualify.

- Other means-tested benefits and tax credits are gradually being replaced. Claimants will be transferred to universal credit over several years.

1. What is universal credit?

Universal credit is a social security benefit for people of working age. It is being introduced in stages throughout Great Britain. It has been available in all areas since the end of April 2016, but only for limited groups of people – this is known as the 'live service'. The 'full service', which is available for all groups of people, is being gradually rolled out and is due to be in all areas for new claimants by

September 2018. Universal credit combines 'means-tested' support for adults, children and housing costs into one benefit.

The existing means-tested benefits and tax credits for working-age people are being replaced by universal credit. This means that once universal credit is fully introduced, if you are, for example, a lone parent, sick or disabled, a carer, unemployed or in low-paid work, and you need help with living expenses, including your rent or mortgage, the means-tested benefit you will claim is universal credit.

2. What is happening to the old benefits system?

Working-age 'means-tested benefits' and tax credits are being gradually replaced with universal credit. However, the old social security system is not going away for some years yet and is not being fully replaced.

What the law says

Benefits and tax credits being replaced

The benefits and tax credits being replaced by universal credit are:

- income support
- income-based jobseeker's allowance
- income-related employment and support allowance
- housing benefit
- child tax credit
- working tax credit

Section 33 Welfare Reform Act 2012

The above benefits are replaced for new claimants as and when universal credit is introduced. You cannot claim these benefits if you have claimed, and are entitled to, universal credit.

If you are already getting one of the old benefits or tax credits, you continue to do so until you claim, or are moved onto, universal credit. There is more information about the transfer to universal credit in Chapter 2.

Universal credit
What you need
to know

WITHDRAWN

Child Pov

Published by Child Poverty Action Group
30 Micawber Street
London N1 7TB
Tel: 020 7837 7979
staff@cpag.org.uk
www.cpag.org.uk
© Child Poverty Action Group 2017

A CIP record for this book is available from the British Library.
ISBN: 978 1 910715 33 8

Child Poverty Action Group is a charity registered in England and Wales (registration
number 294841) and in Scotland (registration number SC039339), and is a company
limited by guarantee, registered in England (registration number 1993854). VAT number:
690 808117

Cover design by Colorido Studios
Typeset by David Lewis XML Associates Ltd
Content management system by KonnectSoft
Printed and bound in the UK by CPI Group (UK) Ltd

Box A
Which benefits remain?
- attendance allowance
- bereavement allowance
- bereavement payment
- bereavement support payment
- carer's allowance
- child benefit
- cold weather payments
- constant attendance allowance
- contribution-based jobseeker's allowance
- contributory employment and support allowance
- disability living allowance
- free school lunches
- funeral payments
- guardian's allowance
- Healthy Start vouchers
- help with health costs
- industrial injuries benefits
- maternity allowance
- pension credit
- personal independence payment
- retirement pension
- school clothing grants
- statutory adoption pay
- statutory maternity pay
- statutory paternity pay
- statutory shared parental pay
- statutory sick pay
- Sure Start maternity grant
- war disablement pension
- war widow's and widower's pension
- widowed parent's allowance
- winter fuel payment

Universal credit does not replace all the current benefits. You can still claim the benefits in Box A after universal credit has been introduced.

Council tax benefit has been abolished, but is not part of universal credit. Instead, local authorities and the Scottish and Welsh governments have responsibility for council tax reduction schemes.

Crisis loans and community care grants from the social fund have also been abolished and replaced by local welfare schemes run by local authorities and the Scottish and Welsh governments.

3. How is universal credit administered?

The **Department for Work and Pensions (DWP)** is responsible for the administration of universal credit. The DWP also deals with the out-of-work benefits that are being replaced and handles the transfer of these claims to universal credit. Different sections within the DWP deal with most of the other benefits that remain outside the universal credit system, but still interact with it. This includes 'contributory benefits', pensions, and disability and carers' benefits.

HM Revenue and Customs (HMRC) administers tax credits, which are being replaced. HMRC receives 'real-time information' on earnings from employers, which is then accessed by the DWP, so that universal credit payments can be automatically adjusted as people's earnings change. Child benefit and guardian's allowance remain the responsibility of HMRC.

Local authorities administer housing benefit, which is being replaced. Existing claims continue until they are transferred to universal credit, a process not expected to complete before 2022. Local authorities continue to deal with housing benefit for older people and with housing costs for people in certain supported accommodation. They also keep their rent officers' functions in the private rented sector, and are responsible for council tax reduction schemes, discretionary housing payments, grants and other financial help.

Work coaches in the jobcentre oversee the 'work-related requirements' you must meet in return for getting universal credit. There is more information about these in Chapter 6.

4. How is universal credit different?

There are a number of differences between universal credit and the old benefits and tax credits system.

- **Monthly assessment and payment periods.** Universal credit is assessed according to your circumstances over a calendar month. Awards are based on your earnings and other income received in a month, and payment is made in one monthly sum. Under the old system, people usually get fortnightly payments of adult benefits and separate four-weekly payments of child tax credit. Because of this change, people claiming universal credit may be offered support with budgeting.

- **Online access.** Universal credit is claimed online. If you are under the 'full service', you manage your claim by signing into an online account. The Department for Work and Pensions (DWP) is working with local services to provide more computers for people to use and more free online access, as well as additional support to develop computer skills. The DWP may allow telephone access in limited circumstances and face-to-face assistance in exceptional cases. There is no paper claim form.

- **No hours rules.** The old system has a variety of rules on the number of hours you can work. These make a difference to your entitlement and the amount of benefit you receive, depending on whether you or your partner work less or more than 16, 24 or 30 hours a week. Under universal credit, all work is permitted, encouraged and, in some cases, required, and earnings are automatically taken into account. Universal credit is designed to allow people to work a few hours a week. For example, unlike tax credits, you can get help with childcare costs in your universal credit, no matter how few hours you work.

- **Work incentives.** Universal credit was first introduced with a defining principle of 'making work pay', with increased work incentives that allow claimants to keep more of their universal credit as their earnings rise. In 2016, however, the work incentives changed. Now not everyone gets a 'work allowance' and, for those who do, the amounts are lower.

- **In-work conditionality.** Universal credit claimants who work part time may be obliged to look for more work. This is not a feature of the old working tax credit system, in which you can qualify if you work a certain number of hours. Universal credit claimants who do not do enough to increase their hours or pay can be given a 'sanction' (a reduction in their benefit).

What CPAG says

Winners and losers

Universal credit was originally described as a benefit that would simplify the social security system and ensure that people were better off in work. However, many households, including disabled people, families with disabled children and larger families, are seeing their entitlement reduced compared with the old system. Also, many are struggling while waiting six weeks or more for their first payment of universal credit.

The government says that people will not be worse off when they are transferred to universal credit, but since universal credit was first planned, cuts to benefits and tax credits have made most families significantly worse off already.

Originally, one positive feature of universal credit was that people could earn more before their universal credit was reduced (the 'work allowance'). However, following a cut to the work allowances, this higher incentive to work was diminished for most people from April 2016, and any increase in the minimum wage cannot fully compensate for their loss.

Universal credit has an increased focus on conditionality and sanctions, making it difficult for people to manage, leaving some people destitute and compelling others into low-paid, insecure work with zero-hour contracts.

These concerns begin to outweigh the positive aspects of universal credit, such as providing more support for childcare costs, and they are exacerbated by the practical difficulties with monthly budgeting and online claims experienced by many families on low incomes.

Chapter 2
When universal credit affects you

This chapter covers:

1. When can you claim universal credit?

2. What happens if your circumstances change?

3. Transfers to universal credit

What you need to know

- People can make a claim for universal credit at different times, depending on their circumstances and the area in which they live.

- While universal credit is available in every area in Great Britain, in some areas only people who meet certain 'gateway' conditions can claim.

- Once you have made a claim and are entitled to universal credit, you usually remain entitled, even if you stop meeting the gateway conditions.

- Universal credit replaces old 'means-tested benefits' and tax credits. If you are entitled to universal credit, you can no longer get these.

- The process of transferring everyone from the old means-tested benefits and tax credits to universal credit is not expected to begin until 2019, and will not be completed until the end of 2022.

1. When can you claim universal credit?

When you can claim universal credit depends on whether you are in a 'full service' area or a 'live service' area. You can check which type of area you live in by entering your postcode at www.universalcreditinfo.net.

Box A

Universal credit areas

- The **'live service'** areas. In these areas, you can make a claim for universal credit if you satisfy the 'gateway' conditions. In most areas you must be single and not have children, but couples and those with children may claim in limited areas.

- The **'full service'** areas. In these areas, there are no gateway conditions and you can claim whatever your circumstances. However, between 6 April 2017 and 31 October 2018 inclusive, if you want to make a new claim and have three or more children, you will be told to claim tax credits instead. If you need to claim other 'means-tested benefits', you will have to claim the old means-tested benefits such as housing benefit, jobseeker's allowance, employment and support allowance or income support. There is more information about this in Chapter 9.

By September 2018, universal credit 'full service' should have been introduced for all new claimants throughout Great Britain. Current claimants of old means-tested benefits and tax credits should then begin to be transferred to universal credit starting in July 2019, and this process should be completed by March 2022.

Unless you live in a 'full service' area, to make a claim for universal credit you must satisfy certain gateway conditions. If you can make a claim as a couple, both of you must satisfy the gateway conditions, unless you have already been getting universal credit as a single person.

The gateway conditions differ slightly, depending on where you live.

Box B
The 'gateway' conditions

You must satisfy all the following main gateway conditions.

- Generally you are single and have no children, although in parts of the north-west of England you can also claim if you are in a couple, and with or without children, provided your child is not certified blind or sight impaired and does not get either disability living allowance or personal independence payment.

- You are a British citizen who has lived in the UK for the last two years, and you have a national insurance number and a bank, building society, Post Office or credit union account.

- You are aged at least 18, but under 60 years and six months.

- You are fit for work.

- You do not have more than £6,000 capital.

- You do not earn (or expect to earn) more than £338 a month (or have more than £541 joint earnings if you are a couple).

- You are not self-employed.

- You are not already getting one of the following benefits:
  - income support (including if you have claimed it and are waiting for a decision on your claim, or if you are appealing)
  - contribution-based and income-based jobseeker's allowance (including if you have claimed it and are waiting for a decision on your claim, or if you are appealing)
  - contributory and income-related employment and support allowance (including if you have claimed it and are waiting for a decision on your claim, or if you are appealing)
  - disability living allowance
  - personal independence payment
  - incapacity benefit
  - severe disablement allowance

- You are not waiting for the outcome of a revision of a decision that you are not entitled to housing benefit.

- You are not pregnant (or within 15 weeks of having given birth), a foster parent or adopting a child (unless the child was placed with you more than a year ago).

- You are not caring for a disabled person.

- You are not a full-time or part-time student or on a training course, or planning to start education or training within one month.

- You are not a homeowner, homeless or living in supported accommodation.

If you can make a claim for universal credit, you must also satisfy the basic rules of entitlement and the financial conditions. There is more information about these in Chapter 3.

How does universal credit affect your other benefits and tax credits?

If you live in a 'full service' area, universal credit replaces means-tested benefits and tax credits for working-age people (unless you are making a new claim and have three or more children). This also applies if you live in a 'live service' area and satisfy the gateway conditions. You cannot get any of the following benefits or tax credits, if you are entitled to universal credit or if you are waiting for a decision on whether you are entitled to it:

- income support
- income-based jobseeker's allowance (but you can get contribution-based jobseeker's allowance as well as universal credit)
- income-related employment and support allowance (but you can get contributory employment and support allowance as well as universal credit)
- housing benefit (except if you are in certain types of 'specified accommodation')
- child tax credit
- working tax credit

In a 'full service' area, you are no longer able to make a new claim for any of these benefits unless you have three or more children. If you are in a 'live service' area, you cannot make a new claim for income-based jobseeker's allowance if you meet the gateway conditions, even if you do not make a claim for universal credit, or if you claim but are not entitled to it. However, depending on your circumstances, you may still be able to get income-related employment and support allowance, income support, housing benefit, child tax credit and working tax credit if you have not claimed universal credit or if you are not entitled to it. **Note:** the rules on this are likely to change over time.

If you get pension credit, you can make a new claim for housing benefit and child tax credit.

Box C
Specified accommodation

This is accommodation where you can get certain types of help or support. It includes:

- accommodation provided by housing associations, charities and some councils where care, support or supervision is provided
- temporary accommodation for people who have left home because of domestic violence

You can get child benefit, personal independence payment and other 'non-means tested benefits' at the same time as universal credit.

Claimants in 'live service' areas who do not meet the gateway conditions can continue to claim the old means-tested benefits and tax credits for the time being.

2. What happens if your circumstances change?

If you live in a 'full service' area and you stop being entitled to universal credit, you still cannot make a new claim for the old 'means-tested benefits' (unless you have three or more children – there is more about this in Chapter 9).

If you live in a 'live service' area and you are claiming universal credit, your entitlement does not stop simply because you no longer meet the 'gateway' conditions – eg, if you become ill and are no longer fit for work.

EXAMPLE

Change of circumstances

Peter lives in a 'live service' area and originally got universal credit as a single unemployed person. However, he becomes ill and is no longer fit for work. He is assessed as having 'limited capability for work'. Although this means that he would not satisfy the 'gateway' conditions if he were making a new claim, he continues to receive universal credit. He is also entitled to a 'limited capability for work element' as part of his universal credit award.

If you originally claimed universal credit as a single person, but then become part of a couple, you are entitled to universal credit as a couple, even if you live in a 'live service' area and no longer satisfy the gateway conditions. However, you must still satisfy the basic rules of entitlement and the financial conditions described in Chapter 3.

If your partner was not entitled to universal credit as a single person but s/he was getting one of the means-tested benefits and tax credits that universal credit replaces, this benefit award stops.

> **EXAMPLE**
>
> **Change of circumstances**
>
> Sam lives in a 'live service' area outside of the north-west of England and has been getting universal credit as a single person. She moves in with her partner Jo and her three-year-old son. Jo has been getting income support, housing benefit and child tax credit as a lone parent. Sam and Jo are now treated as having made a joint claim for universal credit and are entitled to it, even though they do not satisfy the gateway conditions in the area in which they live because they are a couple. Jo's income support, housing benefit and child tax credit all stop.

If your partner is entitled to pension credit, s/he must withdraw her/his pension credit claim in order for you to get universal credit as a couple. So, in this situation, you can choose whether to get universal credit or pension credit. Generally, it is likely that you will be better off claiming pension credit.

Similarly, if you originally claimed universal credit as a couple but then separate from your partner, you can get universal credit as a single person, even if you live in a 'live service' area and no longer satisfy the gateway conditions. You must still satisfy the basic rules of entitlement and the financial conditions described in Chapter 3.

What happens if you are no longer entitled to universal credit?

If your entitlement to universal credit stopped but you think you may be entitled again, you must usually make a new claim. This means that you must be living in a 'full service' area, or in a 'live service' area and you meet the gateway conditions. If you do not, you cannot get universal credit. You may be able to get the old means-tested benefits and tax credits instead.

EXAMPLE

Universal credit stops

Ravinder was getting universal credit, but he became a full-time student and so his entitlement came to an end. However, a few months later, he falls ill and cannot continue studying. He makes another claim for universal credit. As he lives in a 'live service' area and he is not fit for work, he does not satisfy the gateway conditions. He cannot claim universal credit. He may be able to claim any of the old means-tested benefits, including income-related employment and support allowance. He may also be entitled to other benefits, such as contributory employment and support allowance and personal independence payment.

However, if your entitlement to universal credit stops because your earnings are too high, you can reclaim universal credit and you will have the same 'assessment period' and payment dates, provided it is not more than six months since your last day of entitlement. If you live in a 'live service' area, you do not have to make a claim, but if you live in a 'full service' area, you will need to make a rapid reclaim – you only have to give information about anything that has changed since your last claim.

So, in the example above, if Ravinder had stopped getting universal credit because he was working and his earnings were too high rather than because he became a full-time student, he could get universal credit again within six months, even though he is no longer fit for work and does not satisfy the gateway conditions.

3. Transfers to universal credit

From some point, probably starting in July 2019, if you are getting any of the 'means-tested benefits' or tax credits that universal credit replaces, your claim will be transferred to universal credit. Your old benefit or tax credit claim will end.

You will not have to do anything to make the universal credit claim, although you will be expected to notify any changes in your circumstances and whether there is anything incorrect about your new claim. The Department for Work and Pensions refers to this transfer process as 'managed migration'. The process is due to be completed for most people by 2022. However, the arrangements described here may change.

The government's intention is that you should not be financially worse off at the point when your claim is transferred to universal credit. The amount of universal credit you get should therefore not be less than the total amount of your means-tested benefits and tax credits. If it is less, you will get a top-up amount of universal credit (called 'transitional protection') to make up the difference. There is more information on this in Chapter 5.

Further information

The latest area postcodes in which universal credit has been introduced are at www.gov.uk/guidance/government/publications/universal-credit-transition-to-full-service. There is a also a list of jobcentres for the areas in which universal credit has been introduced at www.gov.uk/jobcentres-where-you-can-claim-universal-credit.
To check which benefits are available to whom in a particular area, use the universal credit postcode checker at www.universalcreditinfo.net.

Chapter 3
Who can get universal credit

This chapter covers:

1. Who can get universal credit?

2. What are the basic rules?

3. What are the financial conditions?

4. Other financial help

What you need to know

- To make a new claim for universal credit, you must live in a 'live service' area and meet the 'gateway' conditions that apply in that area, or live in a 'full service' area (and be responsible for fewer than three children or qualifying young people).

- To get universal credit, you must meet the basic rules of entitlement and the financial conditions.

- There are basic rules about your age, residence in Great Britain, whether you are in education and about agreeing to a 'claimant commitment'. This lists what you must do in return for receiving universal credit.

- The financial conditions are about your income and capital (such as savings, investments and certain types of property). You cannot get universal credit if your capital is above £16,000 (although some capital is ignored).

- If you are in a couple, both of you must usually meet the basic rules and the financial conditions.

1. Who can get universal credit?

Universal credit is a benefit for both single people and couples on a low income to provide financial support for living costs, children, housing costs and other needs. You can get universal credit if you are in or out of work.

Currently, however, to make a claim in 'live service' areas you must meet various 'gateway' conditions, and in all areas you cannot make a new claim for universal credit if you have three or more children. Chapters 2 and 9 have more information on this. This chapter does not explain those rules, but instead explains the general rules on who can get universal credit once you are able to make a claim.

You can get universal credit if you meet the basic rules of entitlement and the financial conditions. Provided you meet these, you can get universal credit regardless of your particular circumstances. For example, you can claim if you are:

- a parent, including a lone parent
- ill or disabled
- a carer
- unemployed
- employed or self-employed

EXAMPLES

Who can get universal credit

George has been made redundant. Depending on his income and his other circumstances, he can get universal credit to provide him with some financial help.

Rosie is a lone parent working 12 hours a week in a low-paid job. She has two children and they live in a housing association property. She can claim universal credit to provide her with some financial help.

Your specific circumstances are taken into account to decide how much universal credit you get and what you are expected to do to move towards work. There is more information in Chapter 5 on the amount of universal credit you can get, and in Chapter 6 on the 'work-related requirements' you may need to satisfy.

Couples

If you are in a couple, you normally make a joint claim with your partner. Both of you must usually satisfy the basic rules of entitlement and the financial conditions.

You count as a member of a couple if you are living together and are married or civil partners, or if you are living together as if you were a married couple or civil partners. In some circumstances, you must claim as a single person, even though you are a member of a couple – eg, if your partner is under 18, but you are not. Chapter 4 contains some examples and more information about claiming universal credit.

In two circumstances, it is possible to get universal credit as a couple even though one of you does not meet the basic rules. These are if one of you has reached the qualifying age for pension credit and the other has not, or if one of you is a student and the other is not.

EXAMPLE

One member of a couple is a student

Molly is on a full-time undergraduate course and her partner Mike is unemployed. They have no children. They can claim universal credit as a couple, even though Molly is a student.

If you are a couple and your partner has not accepted a 'claimant commitment', outlining what you must do in order to receive universal credit, but you have, you cannot get universal credit. You must each accept your own claimant commitment to qualify for universal credit if you are a couple. Chapter 6 has more information about the claimant commitment.

Who cannot get universal credit?

Universal credit is being introduced gradually, so in some areas you can only claim it if you meet specific conditions. If you are in a 'full service' area, you can generally claim universal credit if your circumstances change so that you need to submit a new claim for 'means-tested benefits'. However, if you have three or more children, you have to claim tax credits instead, and any of the other 'old' benefits that apply. This is likely to be the case until November 2018. There is more about the 'two-child rule' in Chapter 9. If you are in a 'live service' area you can only claim universal credit if you meet the gateway conditions. There is more information about when universal credit affects you in Chapter 2.

EXAMPLES

Who cannot get universal credit

Louise is a lone parent. Her son is disabled and gets disability living allowance. Her job ends and she needs to claim benefit. She meets the basic rules and financial conditions for universal credit, but cannot claim it because she is in a 'live service' area and does not meet the gateway conditions. She claims income support instead.

Davy is 21 and has recently split up with his partner. He is homeless. He meets the basic rules and financial conditions for universal credit, but cannot claim it because he is in a 'live service' area and does not meet the gateway conditions. He claims jobseeker's allowance instead.

Tom has just moved in with Claire who has three children. Although they live in a 'full service' area and meet the basic rules and financial conditions for universal credit, they cannot claim it because they have more than two children. They claim tax credits instead.

If you are in prison, you can get universal credit for up to six months, but only for your housing costs. You cannot get universal credit if you are fully maintained by a religious order.

2. What are the basic rules?

To be entitled to universal credit, you must meet certain basic rules. There are some exceptions, which are explained in this section.

What the law says

The basic rules

You meet the basic rules for universal credit if:
- you are aged 18 or over
- you are under the qualifying age for pension credit
- you are not in education
- you are resident in Great Britain
- you accept a 'claimant commitment'

Section 4 Welfare Reform Act 2012

EXAMPLE

The basic rules

Jane and Kevin are a British couple, both aged 20. They live in a 'full service' area. Neither are students. Can they claim universal credit?

They meet the age rules, they are in Great Britain and they are not in education, so they can claim universal credit. They must claim jointly as a couple. They must also meet the financial conditions and agree to meet certain 'work-related requirements'. Their income will be compared with the maximum amount of universal credit for their circumstances to see whether they get an award and, if so, how much this will be.

Your age

Are you under 18?

Usually, you must be aged 18 or over to claim universal credit. You can claim at age 16 or 17 if:

- you have a child
- you have a disability and get disability living allowance or personal independence payment and have 'limited capability for work'
- you are 'without parental support'

What the law says

Without parental support

You are without parental support if you are living away from your parents or someone acting in their place because you are estranged from them or because there is a risk to your health, or your parents cannot support you because they are ill, disabled, in prison or not allowed to enter Great Britain, or you are an orphan. This does not apply to you if you are looked after by the local authority, or someone else (such as a grandparent) is acting in place of a parent.

Regulation 8(3) The Universal Credit Regulations 2013

Note: if you claim universal credit for yourself, your parent cannot continue to claim benefit for you, so it may be important to check this before you claim.

Provided you are not a student, you can also get universal credit when you are 16 or 17 if:

- you are pregnant and your baby is due within 11 weeks
- you are ill or disabled and have limited capability for work or you are waiting for a limited capability for work assessment and have provided a 'fit note' from your doctor
- you are a carer – usually, you must also get carer's allowance

If you are a care leaver aged 16 or 17, you can only get universal credit if you have a child, or are ill or disabled. Your universal credit does not include an amount for your housing costs.

Are you over pension credit age?

To get universal credit as a single person, you must be below the qualifying age for pension credit. This is gradually increasing from age 60 and, under current plans, will reach 66 in 2020.

If you are getting universal credit and form a couple with someone over pension credit age, you can currently choose whether to claim pension credit or universal credit. You cannot get both.

EXAMPLE

One member of a couple is over pension credit age

Joan is 58 and gets universal credit. She moves in with her partner Charlie, who is 65 and gets an occupational pension. They claim universal credit as a couple.

Joan must meet work-related requirements as a condition of getting universal credit, but Charlie does not need to.

If Charlie claims pension credit instead, Joan will not need to meet work-related requirements, and it is likely they will be financially better off.

Education

In general, you cannot get universal credit if you are a student. This is called 'receiving education' by the Department for Work and Pensions (DWP). However, there are some exceptions to this.

What the law says

Who is a student

- From your 16th birthday to 1 September after your 19th birthday, you are a student if you are at school or college on a non-advanced course (eg, below degree or Higher National Certificate level) or you are in training that is 'approved' by the DWP.

- You are a student while you are on a full-time course of advanced education – eg, at Higher National Certificate or degree level.

- You are a student while you are on another kind of full-time course, advanced or non-advanced, and you get a loan or grant for your maintenance.

- Even if you are not in one of the above three groups, you count as a student if your course is not compatible with the hours that you are expected to be available for work or with other work-related requirements you are expected to meet for your universal credit claim.

Regulations 5, 12 and 13 The Universal Credit Regulations 2013

Which students can get universal credit?

You can get universal credit while you are student if you are in one of the following groups.

- You have a child.

- You are a single foster parent (including some kinship carers).

- You are a foster parent and your partner is also a full-time student.

- You are disabled and get disability living allowance or personal independence payment and you have been assessed as having limited capability for work.

- You are aged under 22, without parental support, and on a non-advanced course which you started before your 21st birthday.

- You are a member of a couple and your partner is not a student.

- You have taken time out from your course because of illness or caring responsibilities, you have now recovered or your caring responsibilities have now ended, and you are waiting to rejoin your course.

- You are over the qualifying age for pension credit.

How much universal credit you get, if any, depends on your income. Student loans and some grants count as income, but usually only during the academic year. Chapter 5 explains how your universal credit is worked out.

EXAMPLES

Students who can get universal credit

Graham is on a full-time advanced course. He is disabled and gets personal independence payment, and has limited capability for work. Depending on his income, he can claim universal credit.

Lauren is on a full-time advanced course and is a lone parent. Depending on her income, she can claim universal credit.

Residence in Great Britain

In general, you must be resident in Great Britain to claim universal credit, although there are exceptions to this.

Are you going abroad?

You can continue to get universal credit while abroad for up to one month. You must usually continue to meet your work-related requirements. There are only limited circumstances when you can get universal credit for longer than this – eg, for up to two months if a close relative has died or up to six months if the trip is to get medical treatment. If you stay at home and your partner is abroad for longer than a month, the amount of your universal credit usually decreases, so it is important to tell the DWP. Some people who work abroad can get universal credit – eg, members of the armed forces.

Have you come to Great Britain from abroad?

In some cases, if you have come from abroad you cannot get universal credit, even though you are resident in Great Britain.

You cannot usually get universal credit if you are defined as a 'person subject to immigration control'. You will usually have 'no recourse to public funds' stamped in your passport or stated in the document issued to you confirming your leave. This means you cannot claim most social security benefits, including universal credit. People who have refugee leave, humanitarian protection or discretionary leave, and those in some other circumstances, can get universal credit.

You must have a 'right to reside' in Great Britain. If you are a UK national, you have a right to reside. The requirement to have a right to reside mostly affects nationals of countries in the European Economic Area. In most cases, if you are working or self-employed, you have a right to reside. There are other circumstances in which you may also have a right to reside, but being a jobseeker alone is not sufficient for universal credit.

EXAMPLES

Right to reside for universal credit

Natasha is French and a lone parent. She is working full time in Great Britain. She has a right to reside as a worker and can claim universal credit.

Saskia is Lithuanian and a lone parent of a six-month-old baby. She is a full-time student, but has never worked in Britain. She does not have a right to reside and cannot claim universal credit.

You may also have to be 'habitually resident' before you can get universal credit. In broad terms, this means that you have been living here for a while and intend to stay for some time to come.

Accepting a claimant commitment

To be entitled to universal credit, you must normally accept a claimant commitment. This sets out what you must do to receive your universal credit award. The key part of a claimant commitment is about work-related requirements. There is more information about the claimant commitment in Chapter 6.

3. What are the financial conditions?

To be entitled to universal credit, your income must be sufficiently low. How much income you can have and still be entitled to some universal credit depends on your circumstances. Usually, as your income increases, the amount of universal credit you get decreases. If you have a partner, it is your combined income that counts.

Your capital (eg, savings and investments) must not be more than £16,000. If it is higher than £16,000, you are not entitled to universal credit. If you have a partner, it is your combined capital that counts.

There is more information about the income and capital rules in Chapter 5.

You must also meet the basic rules.

4. Other financial help

If you get universal credit, you may be eligible for the following.

- A Sure Start maternity grant. This is a grant (£500 in 2017/18) to help with the costs of a newborn baby, usually only if there is no other child under 16 in your family.

- A funeral expenses payment to cover basic funeral costs.

- A cold weather payment for weeks when the temperature is below freezing.

- Healthy Start vouchers and vitamins. These are currently awarded on a discretionary basis, if take-home pay is less than £408 a month (in 2017/18).

- Free prescriptions, NHS sight tests, vouchers for glasses, dental treatment and fares to hospital. In England, you are only eligible if your monthly earnings are no more than £435, or £935 if you have a child or get an element for 'limited capability for work' or 'limited capability for work-related activity' in your universal credit award.

Under the old benefits system, if you get certain 'means-tested benefits', such as income support, income-based jobseeker's allowance, income-related employment and support allowance or child tax credit, you qualify for other financial help. This is known as 'passporting'.

Other financial help includes:

- free school lunches in Year 3/Primary 4 and above
- school clothing grants
- help with heating and energy efficiency measures
- legal aid
- local leisure facility discounts
- social tariffs from utility companies

Some schemes are administered by central government departments, some by the Scottish and Welsh governments, and some by local authorities or other agencies. Some of this passported help is provided in cash or vouchers, and some by discounts on charges.

In general, you must make a separate claim for the passported help. In some cases, you must receive the necessary out-of-work benefit to qualify, and people not getting the required benefit but who are on a low income are excluded. As universal credit is introduced and these means-tested benefits are abolished, the existing criteria will change, but the government intends that people who would have qualified under the old system remain eligible.

Currently, if you get universal credit, your children can get free school lunches. This may change in the longer term.

Further information

There is more information about who can get universal credit and other benefits you may qualify for in CPAG's *Welfare Benefits and Tax Credits Handbook.*

There is more information about benefits for students in CPAG's *Student Support and Benefits Handbook* and CPAG in Scotland's *Benefits for Students in Scotland Handbook.*

Chapter 4
Claiming universal credit

This chapter covers:

1. Who should claim universal credit?

2. How do you make a claim?

3. When should you claim?

4. How are you paid?

5. Reporting changes in your circumstances

What you need to know

- Couples make a joint claim for universal credit. If you are a lone parent or a single person, you make a single claim.
- The usual way to claim is online, although some people can claim by telephone or in person.
- Universal credit is normally paid directly into your bank account. Couples can have a joint account or choose who should be paid.
- Payments are normally made monthly. Payment for rent is paid to you, not directly to your landlord. There are 'alternative payment arrangements' for people who need help managing their money.
- Unless you are told otherwise, you do not need to report changes in your earnings if your employer is using the 'real-time information' system to report your earnings every time you are paid. You must report any other changes yourself.

1. Who should claim universal credit?

Universal credit is a benefit to provide support for adults and children. If you are single or a lone parent, you claim for yourself as a single person. If you are in a couple, you make a joint claim. In most areas that are under the 'live service', you must be single to claim. Chapter 2 has more information on this.

Usually it is clear whether or not you are in a couple, but there are rules about this.

What the law says

Couples

- You are married and living in the same household.

- You are civil partners and living in the same household.

- You are not married or civil partners, but are 'living together as though you were a married couple or civil partners'.

Section 39 Welfare Reform Act 2012

The Department for Work and Pensions (DWP) decides whether you are living together as a married couple or civil partners by looking at various factors, including whether you have the same address, the type of relationship you have, whether you have children and your financial arrangements.

Claiming jointly means the amount you get is based on your combined income and capital. It also means you must each meet the basic rules of entitlement and have your own 'claimant commitment', setting out the 'work-related requirements' that are expected of you. There is more information about claimant commitments in Chapter 6.

Although usually you claim universal credit jointly as a couple, sometimes only one of you is allowed to claim because the other does not meet the basic rules. In this case, you claim as a single person. This might happen, for example, if your partner is abroad or away from home for an extended period, or does not meet immigration or residence conditions, or if one or both of you are under 18. It is still important to give details about both of you when you claim, because although you may not get any amount for your partner in your award, you are normally still treated as a couple for other parts of the assessment. So, for example, your joint income and capital is taken into account, and your partner's circumstances count when deciding whether you can get any help with childcare costs.

EXAMPLES

Claiming as a single person or as a couple

Eva is 17 and lives with her partner Ryan, who is 18. They are both looking for work. Ryan claims as a single person because Eva is not entitled as a 17-year-old. He gets a 'standard allowance' for himself at the single rate. Because he is claiming as a single person and he is under 35 years old, his 'housing costs element' is restricted to the rate for a room in shared accommodation.

Theo is aged 19. He lives with his 17-year-old partner Johanna and their baby. They make a joint claim because Johanna has a child and so is entitled to universal credit as a 17-year-old.

Frida is a UK national. Her partner Diego is from Brazil. His stay in the UK is subject to immigration conditions. He is allowed to work, but not to have 'recourse to public funds'. Frida claims as a single person. She gets a standard allowance for herself at the single rate and a housing costs element, reduced to take account of Diego's earnings.

What happens if you start or end a relationship?

If you were claiming jointly as a couple but have separated from your partner, tell the DWP. You can then make a fresh claim for universal credit based on your new circumstances. You should claim as soon as possible, but you can ask for your new claim to be backdated, provided you do so within a month of the award stopping. If your former partner has already told the DWP, your own award can be reassessed without your making a fresh claim.

If you become a couple (eg, you and your partner start living together), you do not need to make a new claim, provided at least one of you was getting universal credit already. You must tell the DWP about the change in your situation and give any information required. You should also tell the Tax Credit Office if either of you were getting tax credits. You cannot get tax credits or another 'means-tested benefit' at the same time as universal credit, so these will stop.

Usually when you make a new claim for universal credit, you are not entitled for the first seven 'waiting days'. However, when you become a couple or become single and your universal credit changes to a joint claim or a single claim, you are normally paid on the same day of the month as previously, and there are no waiting days at the start.

Are you unable to make your own claim?

If you cannot make a claim yourself, perhaps because you have a mental health problem or learning disability, someone else (called an 'appointee'), who might be a friend or relative, can be authorised to claim on your behalf. If you have a partner, s/he could make the joint claim for both of you.

2. How do you make a claim?

You claim universal credit:

- online at www.gov.uk/apply-universal-credit
- by telephone if you cannot claim online
- in person, if you cannot make an online or phone claim without assistance

The usual way to claim universal credit is online. The website first checks whether you are in a 'live service' or in a 'full service' area. If you are in a 'live service' area, it checks whether you meet the 'gateway' conditions. If you are eligible to claim, the online instructions take you through the claim. There is a telephone helpline you can use if you need help while you are going through the online claim (0345 600 0723; textphone 0345 600 0743, Monday to Friday 8am to 6pm). This is not a free call.

Box A
Completing the online claim form

- When you are ready to claim, make sure you have the following information to hand:
  - your national insurance number
  - any child benefit reference numbers
  - details of any income that is not from work
  - any other benefits you or your partner get
  - any savings or capital
  - your rent agreement
  - details and registration number of your childcare provider
  - your bank account details

- Completing the claim is likely to take up to 40 minutes.

- If you are in a 'live service' area and claiming as a couple, one of you completes the online claim form entering details for both of you. If you are in a 'full service' area and claiming as a couple, you both need to make an online claim. The first person to claim is given a 'linking code' to give to her/his partner, so that the two claims can be linked together as one.

- When you get to the end of your online claim, you are given a summary of the information you have entered. You have a chance to go back and correct any mistakes. When you are happy that the information is correct, submit your claim.

- If you are in a 'live service' area, your claim is not saved until you submit the form at the end. If you are inactive on the claim for more than 20 minutes, it times out and you have to start again. If you are in a 'full service' area, you are asked to create a username, password and two security questions at the start. Each time you press 'Next' to move onto the next page, that page is saved. If you do not complete your claim in one go, you can sign in again at any time in the next seven days to complete it. You must press submit at the end.

- After you submit your claim, you are shown the amount of universal credit you are likely to get.

After you submit your claim, the Department for Work and Pensions (DWP) phones you to tell you when to attend an interview at the local jobcentre and which documents to take with you. If you are in the 'full service' area, you may receive a text or email asking you to phone the jobcentre and make an appointment.

At the interview, you are asked to confirm your identity and sign a copy of your claim details. You will meet your 'work coach' and agree what you will do next to look for or prepare for work. This goes into your 'claimant commitment', which is a record of what you are expected to do. You must sign this or your claim will be refused.

Are you unable to claim online?

If you do not have online access at home or you are unable to use the internet, your local jobcentre may help or direct you to local organisations that can help you make your claim. Your local authority may provide computers with internet access that you can use – eg, in local libraries.

If you cannot claim online, you can claim by telephone. An adviser takes your details and completes an online claim for you. If you cannot use the telephone, you can ask to claim in person – eg, at a local office or by an adviser visiting you at home. However, this is intended to be exceptional. If you claim by telephone or in person, your claim starts when you first contact the DWP to say you want to claim, so it is important to do so quickly if you cannot claim online.

There is no paper claim form for universal credit.

3. When should you claim?

Universal credit is being introduced gradually across the country. You can only claim when it is available in your area for people in your circumstances. If you are already getting a 'means-tested benefit' or tax credit, you may be transferred to universal credit at a later date. There is more information about when you can claim and about transferring to universal credit in Chapter 2.

There are general rules about making benefit claims that affect when your entitlement can begin. Usually your entitlement starts seven days after you submit your claim, so it is important not to delay. However, it is sometimes possible for a claim to be backdated.

When can your claim be backdated?

Your claim can only be backdated in certain circumstances and for a maximum of one month. If any of the following reasons apply to you and mean that you could not have reasonably claimed earlier, ask the Department for Work and Pensions (DWP) to backdate your claim for up to a month.

• You have a disability.

• You send a medical certificate to say that you could not claim earlier because you were ill.

• You were getting jobseeker's allowance or employment and support allowance which ended, but you were only notified after it ended.

• You could not claim online because the system was not working.

• You were in a couple, but are now claiming as a single person and your former partner did not accept a 'claimant commitment', which meant that your joint claim was refused or stopped.

If you are a couple claiming universal credit jointly, both of you must be in one of these circumstances.

EXAMPLE

Backdating claims

Amina is aged 20 and has just had her first baby. She is a lone parent. A week after the baby is born, she completes the online claim for universal credit. Her award is not backdated and she misses out on a week's money.

EXAMPLES

Backdating claims

Darius has been in hospital after having a heart attack. He is self-employed and has not been able to work for three weeks. When he gets home, he claims universal credit. He asks for it to be backdated and sends in his medical certificate. The DWP accepts that it was not reasonable for him to have claimed earlier and backdates his award.

Joe lost his job on Monday. He needs help to make an online claim for universal credit. As he has no computer himself and is not confident about using one, on Saturday he goes to his daughter's house and with her help submits his online claim. His award is not backdated.

If Joe had telephoned the DWP to ask to claim by phone, his award could have started from the date he called.

Getting your decision

If you are in a 'live service' area, you get a decision letter by post, telling you how your payments are worked out and what to do if you think the decision is wrong. If you are in a 'full service' area, award notices and communications are made via your online journal.

4. How are you paid?

Universal credit is paid directly into your bank or building society account in monthly payments. It is paid in arrears.

From the date you claim (or after seven 'waiting days' if these apply to you), you must wait for one month and up to another seven days to get your first payment. You are then paid on the same day each month after that. If this falls at a weekend or bank holiday, you are paid on the last working day before that. The amount you get does not change with the number of days in the month. Each payment is based on your circumstances in the last monthly 'assessment period'. The day of the month on which your assessment period starts is fixed by your first day of entitlement to universal credit.

Most people have no entitlement to universal credit for the first seven days after they claim. These are called 'waiting days'. They only start once you have made a claim, so it is important not to delay. There are exceptions. For example, you do not have waiting days if you have recently experienced domestic abuse or if you were in prison or on temporary release in the last month. Also, the waiting days do not apply if you or your partner were getting certain benefits, such as jobseeker's allowance or employment and support allowance, before your universal credit claim.

EXAMPLES

When you are paid

Keith is unemployed. He claims universal credit on 4 October. His entitlement starts seven days later, on 11 October. His first monthly assessment period starts on 11 October and ends on 10 November. He gets £317.82, one month's universal credit, paid into his bank account on 17 November and on the 17th of each month after that.

Ingrid left her partner in September because of domestic abuse and is now living with her sister. Ingrid claims universal credit on 4 October. Waiting days do not apply to Ingrid's claim and her first assessment period starts on 4 October and ends on 3 November. She gets £317.82 paid into her bank account on 10 November and on the 10th of each month after that.

If you are in a couple and claiming jointly, all your universal credit is normally paid to one of you. It is up to you to decide whose account it is paid into, or you can have a joint account. If you cannot decide, the Department for Work and Pensions (DWP) can make the decision.

If your partner will not let you have any of the payment, it could be split between you, or all of it paid to you if the DWP decides that it is in your or your child's interest. This is meant to be exceptional to avoid hardship – eg, if there is domestic abuse or if your partner is not managing the household finances properly. You can ask for a 'split payment'. This is one of the 'alternative payment arrangements'.

Are you having difficulty making the money last?

When you claim universal credit, you are offered advice about budgeting. This may be online, by telephone or face to face at a local money advice service. If you need more help, you can ask for alternative payment arrangements by phoning 0345 600 0723 or by talking to your 'work coach' at the jobcentre. There are three main alternative payment arrangements.

• You can be paid twice a month or, very exceptionally, four times a month.

• Your rent can be paid directly to your landlord (which could be at the request of your landlord).

• Your payment can be split between you and your partner.

EXAMPLE

Alternative payment arrangements

Gemma is a lone parent of two children. To find the money to keep up with loan repayments, she has missed rent payments and is now nearly two months in arrears. She suffers from anxiety and depression, and one of her children is not coping well at school. Gemma explains her circumstances to the DWP and asks for her rent to be paid directly to her landlord. This is agreed. Gemma is also signposted to a local money advice service for debt and budgeting advice.

The DWP decides whether you can be paid this way. You cannot appeal if you disagree, but you can give more information about your situation and ask the DWP to reconsider. The decision is based on guidance and depends on your circumstances. The DWP reviews the arrangements after a period of time, usually from three months to two years.

Box B

Alternative payment arrangements

You are most likely to be accepted for an alternative payment arrangement if:

- you have rent arrears or are threatened with eviction or repossession
- you have severe debt problems
- you have difficulty reading or writing, or with simple mathematics
- you have a learning disability or a mental health condition
- you have an alcohol, drug or gambling addiction
- you are under 18 or a care leaver
- you are homeless or in temporary or supported accommodation
- you are (or were) experiencing domestic abuse
- you are a family with multiple or complex needs

There are other reasons given in the government's guidance why someone might have difficulty managing, so it is worth explaining why you need this help.

Do you need money before you are paid?

You might need some money to tide you over while you wait for your first universal credit payment or while you wait for your award to increase after a change of circumstances, such as leaving a job. In these circumstances, you can ask for an advance payment of universal credit. This is known as a 'short-term advance'. If there is a delay on only one part of your claim (eg, if there is still some information or evidence needed to decide how much housing costs to pay), you can ask for the remainder of your universal credit award to be paid in the meantime as a short-term advance. You pay back the advance out of your universal credit award.

The DWP only gives you a short-term advance if it thinks there is a serious risk that your health or safety or the health and safety of your family will be damaged. You cannot appeal if it is refused, but you can provide more information about your situation and ask the DWP to reconsider.

You may be able to get help in a crisis from your local authority's local welfare assistance scheme.

EXAMPLES

Short-term advance

Carmine is a lone parent with one child. She works part time and rents her home. Carmine claims universal credit. She has been asked to provide proof of the rent she pays, but she does not have a rent book and is having trouble getting the evidence she needs from her landlord. Carmine's part-time wages are not enough to feed the family and pay the bills. She asks for a short-term advance. The DWP decides to pay Carmen all her universal credit, except for her housing costs, as a short-term advance, and tells her it will be deducted from the arrears of the amount she is due once the award is decided.

George is single and rents his home. He has just claimed universal credit, he has no savings and his health is not good. His rent is late and his landlord is threatening to take action. George applies for a short-term advance to help him get by until his first payment. The DWP decides to pay him an advance equivalent to half of his monthly award. It will be recovered over his next six monthly payments.

Do you need a loan?

If you need a loan (eg, for a household item you cannot afford or to meet expenses for a new baby or a new job), you can ask for an advance of universal credit. This is called a 'budgeting advance'.

You can ask for a budgeting advance for whatever you need, but if you are refused you cannot appeal. To qualify, you must have been on universal credit (or income support, income-based jobseeker's allowance, income-related employment and support allowance or pension credit) for at least six months, unless you need the advance to help you get work or stay in work. Your earnings and any savings or capital resources must also be below a certain level. The maximum you can get depends on your family size. If you have a child, you can get up to £812 (in 2017/18).

You pay back the advance from your universal credit award each month – usually over a 12-month period. You must pay it back in full before you can get another budgeting advance.

EXAMPLE

Budgeting advance

Emma is a lone parent and is getting universal credit. Her washing machine has broken down and she needs a new one. Instead of buying one with expensive high street credit, she asks for a budgeting advance of her universal credit. She pays this back out of her monthly award over the next 12 months.

Paying universal credit to other people

The DWP can pay part of your universal credit directly to a third party on your behalf. For example, if you have a mortgage, the amount in your universal credit for mortgage interest is paid directly to your lender.

If you rent your home, normally the amount for rent in your universal credit is paid to you as part of your monthly award, not to your landlord. It is paid this way whether you rent from a local authority, housing association or private landlord. However, if you are finding it difficult to budget or are building up rent arrears, the DWP may decide to pay your landlord directly under the alternative payment arrangements. You can also have amounts deducted from your universal credit to repay arrears of fuel bills and other essential services.

5. Reporting changes in your circumstances

It is important to report all the changes the Department for Work and Pensions (DWP) asks you to tell it about and any other change you think might affect your award. Phone the universal credit helpline on 0345 600 0723 to report changes. This is not a free call, unless it is part of your call package with your phone provider. It is best to report the change in writing as well, if you can. If you are in a 'full service' area, you can use your online journal to notify changes of circumstances.

You will get a letter to confirm the change and tell you how your award is affected. If you are in a 'full service' area, you are notified online.

If you are employed, you do not normally need to report changes in your earnings. The DWP gets information on your earnings from HM Revenue and Customs (HMRC) through its 'real-time information' system. Under this, your employer sends HMRC information about your earnings every time you are paid. However, you may be asked to report your earnings if, for example, your employer is not doing so properly or a report is missing or wrong.

If you are self-employed, you are expected to report your earnings every month on a 'cash in/cash out' basis – ie, the income you have received during the month and payments you have made for that month if they come under set categories.

If you pay for childcare, you may be asked to report your childcare charges each month.

EXAMPLE

Reporting self-employed earnings

Matt is self-employed. He gets a message from the DWP reminding him to report his earnings for 12 February to 11 March (his monthly 'assessment period'). Matt is busy and does not get round to it. His universal credit award is not paid when it is next due and the DWP tells him it has been suspended. He must send in the missing earnings report quickly, otherwise his award will stop altogether.

How do changes affect your award?

You are paid a month in arrears, so every payment you get is based on your circumstances in the previous month. When you report a change in your circumstances, you must wait until your next usual universal credit payday before your award goes up or down. The revised amount is normally worked out as though your new circumstances had lasted for the whole of the previous month. A 'month' means the monthly assessment period on which your payment is based. You are paid a few days after the end of the assessment period and are expected to report any changes before the end of that period.

If you are late reporting a change (being late means that you report it after the end of the assessment period in which the change took place), and your award increases because of the change, you do not get arrears paid before the month you actually reported it, so you will lose money. The DWP can backdate an increased award if there are special circumstances, so it is always worth saying why you are reporting a change late and explaining any difficulties you had, such as ill health.

EXAMPLES

How changes affect awards

Poonam has a new baby on 20 June 2017. This is two weeks into her universal credit assessment period, which ends on 5 July. She tells the DWP on 1 July. Her next payment on 12 July includes an extra £231.67 which is the 'child element' for the whole month in which the baby is born.

Danni has a new baby on 10 July 2017. This is one week into her universal credit assessment period, which ends on 2 August. She is depressed and tired and does not call the DWP until 5 August. She is paid her usual amount on 9 August with no extra for the baby. She is paid an extra £231.67 for the baby on 9 September. She has lost a month's extra money. If Danni had explained why she was late reporting the birth, the DWP could have decided to pay another £231.67 for the first month.

Steve starts university on 6 October. This is three weeks into his universal credit assessment period, which ends on 14 October. He tells the DWP on 6 October. He is no longer entitled to universal credit as a student and so his award stops. On his next payday on 21 October, he gets no universal credit.

If your award decreases because of the change, this is backdated. So, if you are late reporting the change, you have an overpayment. The later you report the change, the more you must pay back. It is possible that you might be asked to pay a fine as well. There is more about fines in Chapter 7.

Further information

The DWP has produced a basic guide *Universal Credit and You* at www.gov.uk/ government/publications/universal-credit-and-you. There is more detailed guidance at www.gov.uk/guidance/universal-credit-toolkit-for-partner-organisations.
You can find details on your local authority's local welfare assistance scheme using CPAG's online postcode finder at www.cpag.org.uk/lwas.
There is more information about universal credit claims and payments in CPAG's *Welfare Benefits and Tax Credits Handbook*.

Chapter 5
The amount of universal credit

This chapter covers:

1. What is the maximum amount of universal credit?

2. How do your income and capital affect universal credit?

3. How much universal credit do you get?

What you need to know

- Universal credit includes an amount for you and your partner. This is called the 'standard allowance'.

- Amounts for children for whom you are responsible are added to the standard allowance. These are called 'child elements'.

- There are additional amounts if your child is disabled.

- Extra amounts are added to the standard allowance, depending on your circumstances. You may get an additional amount if you or your partner are ill or disabled, or if you or your partner are caring for a disabled person. There are also amounts for rent and mortgage costs, and for childcare costs.

- If you have other income, this reduces the amount of universal credit to which you are entitled, although some income is ignored.

- You are not entitled to universal credit if you and your partner have more than £16,000 capital.

1. What is the maximum amount of universal credit?

Universal credit is a 'means-tested benefit'. This means that the amount you get depends on your family circumstances and on how much other income (if any) you have. As your income increases, the amount of your universal credit award reduces.

Your 'maximum universal credit' is made up of the total of a 'standard allowance' and amounts (called 'elements') for:

- each child (limited to two in some circumstances)
- each disabled child (at a lower or higher rate)
- an ill or disabled adult
- you or your partner if you care for a disabled person
- your housing costs
- your childcare costs

Each of these amounts has its own qualifying conditions. The rest of this section explains when these amounts apply and how your maximum amount of universal credit is worked out. There are examples on page 57. If you have no income or your income is below a certain level, you get the maximum amount of universal credit.

The standard allowance

Universal credit includes an amount for you and your partner. This is called the 'standard allowance'. How much you get depends on whether you are making a claim as a single person or a joint claim with your partner, and whether you are aged under 25.

Monthly rates of standard allowance, 2017/18	
Single claimant, under 25	£251.77
Single claimant, 25 or over	£317.82
Joint claimants, both under 25	£395.20
Joint claimants, at least one 25 or over	£498.89

Child element

If you are responsible for any children, your universal credit includes an additional amount (called a 'child element') for each child under

16, and for each 'qualifying young person' who is 16 to 18 (or 19 in some cases) and, for example, is still at school or college on a non-advanced course.

However, from April 2017 a 'two-child limit' applies and you do not get a child element for a 'third or subsequent child' born on or after 6 April 2017. Between 6 April 2017 and 31 October 2018, you cannot make a claim for universal credit if you are responsible for more than two children. Instead, you are directed to claim tax credits and any of the old means-tested benefits that you qualify for. If you are already claiming universal credit and a third or subsequent child joins your household on or after 6 April 2017, you do not receive an amount for that child unless an exception applies. There is more information about the two-child limit and the exceptions in Chapter 9. If the child or young person is disabled, you can still receive the extra amount for a disabled child.

EXAMPLE

Making a claim for three children

Samara has three children and has not claimed universal credit before. She cannot make a claim for universal credit before 1 November 2018 and claims for tax credits instead.

From 1 November 2018, all families will be able to make a new claim for universal credit but a child element will only be paid for the first two children in the family, regardless of when they were born, unless an exception applies.

Monthly rates of child element, 2017/18	
First child/qualifying young person if born before 6 April 2017	£277.08
Each other child/qualifying young person	£231.67

Only one person (or, in a joint claim, one couple) can claim universal credit for a particular child. If a child normally lives with more than one person (eg, if you are separated from your partner and your child lives with both of you), the person who has the main responsibility for the child can claim universal credit for her/him.

You cannot normally be 'responsible' for a child if s/he is being 'looked after' by the local authority. The exceptions to this are if the child is living with you and you have parental responsibility for her/him, or if s/he is being is looked after because s/he is away for a planned short respite break.

Additional amount if your child is disabled

If your child is disabled, your universal credit includes an additional amount. There are two levels of payment, depending on the severity of your child's disability.

- You get the lower amount if your child gets disability living allowance or personal independence payment.

- You get the higher amount if your child gets the highest rate of disability living allowance care component, the enhanced rate of personal independence payment daily living component, or is certified as severely sight impaired or blind.

Monthly additional amounts for a disabled child, 2017/18	
Lower amount	£126.11
Higher amount	£372.30

Even if you do not get the child element for your child because of the two-child limit, you still get the additional amount if s/he is disabled.

Additional amount if you or your partner are ill or disabled

If you or your partner are ill or disabled, you may get an additional amount added to your standard allowance if you are assessed as having 'limited capability for work-related activity'. Before 3 April 2017, a lower additional amount could also be added to your standard allowance if you were assessed as having 'limited capability for work'. Generally, if your period of limited capability for work started on or after 3 April 2017, the 'limited capability for work' element is not included in your maximum award.

Monthly additional amounts for ill health or disability, 2017/186	
Limited capability for work element (only if your limited capability for work started before 3 April 2017)	£126.11
Limited capability for work-related activity element	£318.76

Box A
Limited capability for work test

'Limited capability for work' is a test of whether your health problems or disabilities mean that you are currently unable to work. The assessment normally involves you filling in a questionnaire and attending a medical examination. To pass the test you need to score 15 points on a list of specified activities unless you are treated as having limited capability for work – see Box B. You are likely to be assessed regularly to check whether you still meet these conditions. If you do not return the questionnaire about your health problems or do not attend the medical without a good reason, you are likely to be treated as not satisfying the conditions. The test is also used to decide whether you qualify for employment and support allowance. If you get employment and support allowance, you do not need to have a separate assessment for universal credit. Although there is no additional amount for limited capability for work for new claims from 3 April 2017, it can be important to be assessed as having limited capability for work as it entitles you to work allowances and reduces your level of conditionality.

In some circumstances, you are treated as having limited capability for work without having to be assessed. For example, this applies if you are a hospital patient (this can be extended from when you leave hospital until you have recovered) or you are in residential rehabilitation for drug or alcohol problems. It also applies if you are at least the qualifying age for pension credit and get disability living allowance or personal independence payment.

> Box B
> **Limited capability for work-related activity test**
>
> The severity of your health problems is decided by looking at whether or not you have 'limited capability for work-related activity'. This test is designed to identify whether your illness or disability is so serious that, currently, you should not be expected to think about returning to work. To pass the test you need to meet one of a list of specified descriptors unless you are treated as having limited capability for work-related activity – see below. You may be regularly assessed to check whether you still meet these conditions. If you get employment and support allowance, you do not need to have a separate assessment for universal credit.

In some circumstances, you are treated as having limited capability for work-related activity without having to be assessed. For example, this applies if you are terminally ill or you are having chemotherapy or radiotherapy for cancer, or are likely to do so in the next six months, or if you are recovering from this treatment. It also applies if you are at least the qualifying age for pension credit and get attendance allowance, the highest rate of the disability living allowance care component or the enhanced rate of the daily living component in personal independence payment.

Usually, you do not get an additional element in your universal credit straight away. There is usually a 'waiting period' of at least three months. If you are are terminally ill, and in some other circumstances, there is no waiting period.

If both you and your partner have limited capability for work and/or limited capability for work-related activity, you only get one element. You get the higher element that applies. You cannot get the limited capability for work element or the limited capability for work-related activity element in addition to the 'carer element'. You get the highest one that applies. However, if you are in a couple, one of you can qualify for this element and the other can qualify for the carer element.

If you are getting either the limited capability for work or limited capability for work-related activity element and you start work, you do not automatically lose the element, but your capability may be reassessed. **Note:** if you are already in work and your weekly earnings are at least 16 times the national minimum wage, you can only be newly assessed to get these elements if you get disability living allowance, personal independence payment or attendance allowance.

Additional amount if you or your partner are a carer

If you are caring for someone who is severely disabled, you may get an additional amount added to your standard allowance. This is called the 'carer element'.

Monthly rates of carer element, 2017/18	
Carer element	£151.89

You can get the carer element if you are caring for a severely disabled person for at least 35 hours a week. The person you care for must get attendance allowance, the middle or highest rate of disability living allowance care component, or either rate of the personal independence payment daily living component. The easiest way to qualify is to claim carer's allowance, which is another benefit for carers. However, even if you do not get carer's allowance, you can still get the carer element if you care for the person for at least 35 hours a week. Only one person can get the carer element for a disabled person, even if more than one person is caring for her/him.

If both you and your partner satisfy the rules for the carer element, you get two elements, but not if you are both caring for the same disabled person.

You cannot get the limited capability for work element or the limited capability for work-related activity element in addition to the carer element. You get the highest one that applies. However, if you are in a couple, one of you can qualify for the carer element and the other can qualify for the limited capability for work or limited capability for work-related activity element.

> **EXAMPLE**
>
> **One member of a couple is ill, the other is a carer**
>
> Jim has cancer and is recovering from chemotherapy. Barbara is looking after him. Jim gets personal independence payment. Their universal credit includes a limited capability for work-related activity element of £318.76 and a carer element of £151.89 a month.

Housing costs element

Universal credit can include an amount for certain housing costs. This is called the 'housing costs element'. The housing costs element can cover rent, mortgage interest and some service charges. It usually only covers the housing costs for the home you live in. However, in certain situations, it can be paid for a home you are not living in. For example, if you are prevented from moving into a new home because you are waiting for disability adaptations to be carried out, the housing costs element can be included for up to one month before you actually move in.

There are also limited situations in which you can receive a housing costs element for two homes. For example, if you are disabled and you are waiting for a new home to be adapted, it can be paid for two homes for up to one month. If you are fleeing domestic violence and are living in temporary accommodation but intend to return home, the housing costs element can be paid on both homes for up to 12 months.

Sometimes, despite living in the property, you cannot get a housing costs element – eg, if you are paying rent to a close relative and you are also living with her/him.

From 1 April 2017, most 18–21 year olds who are out of work and subject to all work-related requirements, who make a new claim in a 'full service' area, are not able to get the housing costs element.

Note: the rules on housing costs may be different in Scotland at some point in the future.

Help with your rent
The amount included in your universal credit to help you with your rent depends on how many people are in your family and on your circumstances.

If you are renting from a local authority or housing association, the amount of the housing costs element is based on the rent you pay, plus certain service charges. However, the amount may be restricted if you are considered to be living in a property that is too big for you, or you have a 'non-dependant' living with you. This is often called the 'bedroom tax'. See Box C for how many bedrooms you are allowed.

Box C
How many bedrooms are you allowed?

You are allowed one bedroom for each of the following:

- a couple
- someone aged 16 or over
- two children of the same sex
- two children aged under 10
- any other child
- a carer (or carers) providing overnight care to a disabled child or adult

You may be allowed an additional bedroom if, for example, you have a child with a disability, you are a couple but cannot share a room with your partner because of a disability, or you are a foster carer.

If you have one more bedroom than you are allowed, your housing costs element is reduced by 14 per cent of your rent. If you have two or more additional bedrooms, your housing costs element is reduced by 25 per cent of your rent.

If you live in certain types of 'specified accommodation', you do not get a housing costs element, but you can get housing benefit instead. This includes accommodation where you receive care, support or supervision. Chapter 2 explains who is affected by this.

EXAMPLE

Housing costs element

Tess is a lone parent with two children – a boy aged 10 and a girl aged 12. She is allowed three bedrooms under the universal credit rules. Her housing association house has four bedrooms and her monthly rent is £400. Her housing costs element is reduced by 14 per cent of her rent (£56). Her housing costs element is £344 (£400 – £56).

If you are renting from a private landlord, the amount of the housing costs element is limited to the 'local housing allowance' in your area for the size of property you are assessed as needing.

The number of bedrooms you are allowed is the same as in Box C, except that there is a maximum of four.

If you are single, aged under 35 and have no dependants, you are usually only eligible for a housing costs element to cover the rent for a room in shared accommodation.

The amount of the housing costs element you get to help with your rent (whether you rent from a local authority, housing association or private landlord) is reduced if you have any non-dependants living with you. A non-dependant is someone like an adult son or daughter, or a relative, who shares your home. A set amount of £70.06 a month (in 2017/18) for each non-dependant is deducted from the element, even if you do not receive any contribution from that person. However, there are some situations in which no amount is deducted – eg, if you or the non-dependant are getting the middle or highest rate of disability living allowance care component, or the personal independence payment daily living component, or if your non-dependant is under 21.

If the amount of your universal credit does not cover the full cost of your rent, you may be able to get a discretionary housing payment from your local authority to make up the difference.

Help with your mortgage interest

If you own your home, you may get help with your mortgage interest and with certain service charges. However, you do not get help if you are doing any paid work, no matter how few hours.

You do not normally get any help with your housing costs during the first nine months of your claim for universal credit. You may be able to get help earlier if you were already on income support, employment and support allowance or jobseeker's allowance before getting universal credit. Also, if the housing costs element has stopped being included in your universal credit (eg, because you have started work), you must wait nine months after stopping work before it can be included again.

The amount of your housing costs element is not based on what you pay, but is calculated by using a standard interest rate. The maximum amount of loan that the housing costs element can be paid for is £200,000 (in 2017/18).

Note: in future, help with mortgage interest is likely to be offered as a repayable loan. The government has announced that it intends to make this change from April 2018. However, the rules had not been finalised at the time this book was written.

Childcare costs element

Your universal credit can include an amount for your childcare costs (the 'childcare costs element') if you are in paid work (or are about to start paid work) and you are paying for formal childcare, such as a registered childminder, nursery or after-school club.

You must be:

- a lone parent
- a couple and both of you are working
- a couple and one of you is working and the other has limited capability for work (see Box A), is caring for a disabled person or is temporarily away from home

You are treated as working if you are getting statutory sick pay, maternity allowance or statutory maternity, adoption, paternity or shared parental pay.

You can get this element no matter how few hours you are working. However, the childcare costs must be necessary to enable you to take up, or continue in, paid work or to enable you to maintain your childcare arrangements allowing you to return to work – eg, after maternity leave.

The childcare costs element in 2017/18 is 85 per cent of your actual childcare costs, up to a maximum of £646.35 a month for one child and £1,108.04 for two or more children.

EXAMPLES

Childcare costs element

Amara is a lone parent with one child. She is working and has childcare costs of £600 a month. Amara gets £510 a month childcare costs element in her maximum universal credit amount – ie, 85 per cent of £600.

Ffion and Darren have two children and both work. Their childcare costs are £1,200 a month. They get £1,020 a month childcare costs element in their maximum universal credit amount – ie, 85 per cent of £1,200.

EXAMPLES

Maximum universal credit

Michael and Sharmani are a couple aged 45 and 46 with two children under 10 (born before 6 April 2017). None of the family have health problems. The couple live in a two-bedroom local authority flat with a monthly rent of £300. They have no childcare costs.

Standard allowance £498.89

Child element x two £508.75

Housing costs element £300

Maximum universal credit = £1,307.64

Marcia is a lone parent aged 30 with one child (born before 6 April 2017). She lives in a three-bedroom housing association house and her rent is £350 a month. The house has one more bedroom than Marcia is allowed, so her housing costs element is reduced by 14 per cent of the rent. Marcia's child has a disability and gets the lowest rate of disability living allowance care component. She pays £200 a month for childcare.

Standard allowance £317.82

Child element £277.08

Amount for disabled child £126.11

Housing costs element £301

Childcare costs element £170

Maximum universal credit = £1,192.01

Note: in both examples, if the eldest child was born on or after 6 April 2017, the child element for that child would be reduced.

2. How do your income and capital affect universal credit?

If you and your partner have any income or capital, your universal credit may be affected. Your income could be your earnings or other income, such as other benefits. Your capital includes savings and some property. As your income increases, the amount of universal credit you get usually decreases. Income belonging to your children is ignored.

Your earnings

Your net earnings from employment or self-employment may affect the amount of universal credit you get. 'Net earnings' means your earnings after deducting tax, national insurance and any contribution to an occupational pension scheme.

Your employer is required to report your earnings every month. This is called 'real-time information'. If your earnings are reported by your employer in this way, the figure used in the universal credit assessment is taken from the amount in the reports received by the Department for Work and Pensions (DWP). If your employer does not report your earnings in time, the DWP may ask you to give this information instead.

The earnings figure used in the universal credit calculation is the amount you received in each universal credit 'assessment period', which is one calendar month.

EXAMPLE

Earnings figure

Bert's first universal credit assessment period starts on 8 July 2017. Each assessment period after that starts on the 8th of the month. In the first assessment period (from 8 July to 7 August), he has earnings which are paid on 25 July. This is the earnings figure used to calculate his universal credit for the period 8 July to 7 August. It does not matter what period his earnings are for; it is when they are paid to him that matters.

Chapter 4 has more information on assessment periods.

If you are self-employed, you must report your income and expenses monthly to the DWP. There is a special online tool for this. Expenses can include regular costs like rent or wages, purchase of stock and utility bills. Flat-rate amounts are made for some expenses, such as mileage.

However, if you are self-employed and on a low income, you may be assumed to have a higher income than you do. Normally, unless you are starting a new business, you are treated as earning at least the national minimum wage for someone of your age for the number of hours the DWP expects you to search for work. This is called the 'minimum income floor'. However, if you are not working regularly (eg, because there is little work available or you are unwell), this may indicate that you are not in 'gainful self-employment' and you should not be treated as having income that you do not have.

Statutory sick pay and statutory maternity, paternity, shared parental and adoption pay count as earnings.

If you have a child, or if you or your partner have 'limited capability for work', a 'work allowance' is deducted from your earnings before they reduce your universal credit. The level of the work allowance depends on whether you have a 'housing costs element' included in your universal credit. A household can only have one work allowance, even if you are a couple and both of you have earnings.

Amount of monthly work allowance, 2017/18	
Universal credit includes a housing costs element	£192
Universal credit does not include a housing costs element	£397

EXAMPLES

Work allowance

Jon and Barry are a couple with two children. They have a housing costs element included in their universal credit award. Their work allowance is £192.

Ruby is single and has no children. She has limited capability for work. She has no housing costs element included in her universal credit award. Her work allowance is £397.

Florence is a lone parent with one child. She has a mortgage but because she is working there is no housing costs element included in her universal credit award. Her work allowance is £397.

How do your earnings affect universal credit?

If the work allowance applies to you, deduct this from your earnings. The rest of your earnings count for universal credit and your 'maximum universal credit' is reduced by a proportion of this figure. This is often called the 'taper' – ie, the rate at which your universal credit tapers away as your earnings increase. The taper is 63 per cent. This means that as your earnings increase above the level of any work allowance, your universal credit decreases by 63 pence for every extra pound you earn. If you do not have a work allowance, your universal credit is reduced by 63 pence for every pound you earn. There are examples of how this works on pages 65 and 66.

Do you have other income?

Only certain types of other income are taken into account for universal credit. For example, the following counts:

- occupational and personal pensions
- certain benefits, including jobseeker's allowance and employment and support allowance
- maintenance for you or your spouse or partner, but not child maintenance
- student loans and some grants

- certain insurance payments
- income from an annuity or certain trusts

Disability living allowance, personal independence payment, attendance allowance, bereavement support payment, war pensions and child benefit are not taken into account as income. Nor is income from lodgers.

Income (other than earnings) which is taken into account reduces your maximum universal credit pound for pound.

Do you have any capital?

Any capital you have may affect your universal credit. 'Capital' includes savings, stocks and shares, property and trusts. Certain types of capital are ignored – eg, property which is your main home, personal injury payments placed in a trust fund, some other compensation payments and, for at least six months, your former home which you are trying to sell. Any capital owned by your children is ignored. If you and your partner have capital of over £16,000 (in 2017/18), you cannot get universal credit.

You are treated as still having capital if you deliberately get rid of it in order to get universal credit or to increase the amount of universal credit you get. This does not apply if you have used the capital to reduce or pay a debt, or to pay for goods or services which are considered reasonable.

Assumed income from capital

If your capital is over £6,000 but £16,000 or less, you are treated as having an income of £4.35 a month for every £250 (or part of £250) over £6,000, regardless of whether you actually receive this income – eg, in the form of interest on your savings.

EXAMPLE

Income from capital

Niamh has £7,400 savings. This is £1,400 over £6,000. She is treated as having an income from this capital of £26.10 a month (£4.35 for every £250, or part of £250, over £6,000). This income reduces her maximum universal credit pound for pound.

3. How much universal credit do you get?

How do you calculate universal credit?

Follow the steps below to work out your entitlement. Universal credit is worked out on a month-by-month basis.

Note: the 'benefit cap' can affect the amount of universal credit you get. There is more information on this on page 67.

Step one: calculate your maximum universal credit
Add together your 'standard allowance', any additional amounts because you have children, any additional amounts for special circumstances (such as the 'limited capability for work-related activity element', 'carer element' or 'childcare costs element') and any 'housing costs element'. The total is your 'maximum universal credit'.

If you have no other income, this is the amount of universal credit you get.

If you have other income, go to Step two.

Step two: work out your income, other than earnings
Your income might include other benefits (such as contributory employment and support allowance), an occupational pension or income from capital. Remember that some benefits, including disability living allowance, personal independence payment and child benefit, are ignored. Your income is worked out on a monthly basis.

Step three: work out your earnings and how much can be ignored
Work out your net earnings received for the month after tax, national insurance and any contribution you make to an occupational pension have been deducted. If you are an employee, this is usually the amount reported by your employer through the 'real-time infomation' system, so normally it is the same as the information on your payslip. If you are self-employed, you may be treated as having higher earnings than you actually have.

Check whether a 'work allowance' applies to you and, if so, deduct it from your net earnings.

Calculate 63 per cent of the resulting figure.

Step four: calculate your total income
Add together the income to be taken into account in Steps two and three.

Step five: calculate your universal credit entitlement
Deduct your total income to be taken into account (Step four) from your maximum universal credit (Step one).

This is the amount of universal credit you get.

EXAMPLE

Lone parent with two children

Sophia is aged 30. She lives in a housing association rented property and is not subject to the 'bedroom tax'. Her rent is £480 a month. She does not have any health problems and she is not looking after a severely disabled person. Her two children, who were both born before 6 April 2017, do not have any disabilities. She has no other income apart from child benefit. Her monthly universal credit is calculated as follows.

Step one: calculate your maximum universal credit
Standard allowance £317.82

Child element x two £508.75

Housing costs element £480

Total = £1,306.57

Sophia has no income apart from child benefit, which is disregarded. She therefore gets the maximum amount of universal credit (£1,306.57). She does not need to follow the remaining steps.

EXAMPLE

Couple with one child

Rob and Gwen are aged 31 and 32. They live in a local authority flat and do not have any 'spare' bedrooms. Their rent is £300 a month. Their child, who born before 6 April 2017, has a disability and receives the lowest rate care component of disability living allowance. Their only other income is child benefit and contributory employment and support allowance of £316.77 a month, which Rob has been getting since May 2017 because he has 'limited capability for work'. Their monthly universal credit is calculated as follows.

Step one: calculate your maximum universal credit
Standard allowance £498.89

Child element £277.08

Disabled child addition £126.11

Housing costs element £300

Total = £1,202.08

Step two: work out your income, other than earnings
Employment and support allowance £316.77 (disability living allowance and child benefit are disregarded)

Step three: work out your earnings and how much can be ignored
Rob and Gwen do not have any earnings.

Step four: calculate your total income
Their total income is £316.77.

Step five: calculate your universal credit entitlement
£1,202.08 − £316.77 = £885.31

EXAMPLE

Single person

Imran is aged 24. He is single and has no children. He has a disability and receives the standard rate of the daily living component and the enhanced rate of the mobility component of personal independence payment. He has limited capability for work which began after 3 April 2017. He lives in a housing association flat. He is not subject to the 'bedroom tax'. His rent is £400 a month. Imran has net earnings of £416 a month. His monthly universal credit is calculated as follows.

Step one: calculate your maximum universal credit
Standard allowance £251.77

Housing costs element £400

Total = £651.77

Step two: work out your income, other than earnings
Personal independence payment is disregarded and, therefore, Imran has no income other than his earnings.

Step three: work out your earnings and how much can be ignored
Imran has £416 a month net earnings.

The work allowance that applies to Imran is £192.

£416 – £192 = £224

£224 x 63% = £141.12

Step four: calculate your total income
Imran's total income is £141.12

Step five: calculate your universal credit entitlement
£651.77 – £141.12 = £510.65

EXAMPLE

Couple with one child

Carl and Meg are a couple aged 30 and 29, with one child who was born on 5 May 2017. Meg works and earns £700 net a month. Carl is on contributory employment and support allowance of £475.15 a month because he has 'limited capability for work-related activity'. Their only other income is child benefit. They live in a housing association house. The rent is £450 a month. The 'bedroom tax' does not apply. They have no childcare costs. Their universal credit is calculated as follows.

Step one: calculate your maximum universal credit
Standard allowance £498.89

Child element £231.67

Limited capability for work-related activity element £318.76

Housing costs element £450

Total = £1,499.32

Step two: work out your income, other than earnings
Carl's employment and support allowance of £475.15 counts in full as income.

Step three: work out your earnings and how much can be ignored
Meg has £700 a month net earnings.

The work allowance that applies to Meg and Carl is £192.

£700 – £192 = £508

£508 x 63% = £320.04

Step four: calculate your total income
£475.15 contributory employment and support allowance plus £320.04 earnings = £795.19

Step five: calculate your universal credit entitlement
£1,499.32 – £795.19 = £704.13

Are you being transferred to universal credit?

If you are getting one of the benefits being replaced because of the introduction of universal credit, you will usually stay on that benefit until the Department for Work and Pensions (DWP) decides to transfer your claim to universal credit. This process is not expected to begin until 2019. Chapter 2 has more information on the transfer process and on when you can make a claim for universal credit yourself.

Once your claim has been transferred, your universal credit may include an additional amount of 'transitional protection'. This ensures that the amount you get when you move onto universal credit is not less than the amount you were getting on your previous benefits. The amount of your universal credit, including the transitional protection, remains the same, without any increases (provided your circumstances do not change), until the normal universal credit amounts catch up over time.

You only get this transitional protection if your claim is transferred by the DWP, not if you can claim universal credit yourself or because of a change in circumstances.

It is expected that your transitional protection will end completely if there is a significant change in your circumstances – eg, if a partner leaves or joins your household, you or your partner stop work or your universal credit award ends. However, the rules on transitional protection had not been finalised at the time this book was written.

The benefit cap

The 'benefit cap' restricts your benefit entitlement to a level set by the government. In 2017/18, the cap is £1,284.16 (inside Greater London) or £1,116.67 (outside Greater London) a month if you are single with no dependent children, and £1,916.67 (inside Greater London) or £1,666.67 (outside Greater London) a month otherwise.

Your 'benefit entitlement' includes universal credit and most other benefits, but does not include pension credit or retirement pension. If your benefit entitlement is more than the cap level, the excess is deducted from your universal credit. If you have a childcare costs element included in your universal credit, this amount is deducted from the excess before your universal credit is reduced. If the childcare costs element is more than the excess, no deduction is made.

Are you exempt from the benefit cap?

You may be exempt from the benefit cap. This includes if:

- you are getting personal independence payment, disability living allowance, attendance allowance or industrial injuries disablement benefit
- your child gets disability living allowance or personal independence payment
- you have limited capability for work-related activity
- you are a war pensioner, or a war widow/widower
- you earn an amount equal to working 16 hours a week at the national living wage converted to a net monthly amount – the 'earnings exception threshold'

If you have been working for a year or more earning at least the earnings exception threshold and you stop working, you are exempt from the benefit cap for nine months.

Further information

You can check the local housing allowance that applies to you at https://lha-direct.voa.gov.uk/search.aspx.

There is more information about universal credit amounts, and how income and capital is worked out, in CPAG's *Welfare Benefits and Tax Credits Handbook*.

Chapter 6
Your claimant commitment

This chapter covers:

1. What is the claimant commitment?

2. What are you expected to do?

3. Who must look for work?

4. Who must prepare for work?

5. Who must take part in work-focused interviews?

6. Who has no work-related requirements?

What you need to know

- When you claim universal credit, you must accept a 'claimant commitment'.

- If you claim as a couple with your partner, s/he must also accept a claimant commitment.

- Your claimant commitment lists your 'work-related requirements' while getting universal credit. These vary from being immediately available for and searching for full-time work to having no requirements.

- If you already work, you may be expected to look for more work or better paid work, if your earnings are low.

1. What is the claimant commitment?

When you claim universal credit, you must normally accept a 'claimant commitment' before you can get any benefit. If you have a partner, you must both accept an individual commitment. What is in your claimant committment is decided after an interview with your Department of Work and Pensions (DWP) 'work coach'. It should take into account any health issues or caring commitments that you have. Your claimant commitment can be be changed or updated if your circumstances change. If it is changed, you must accept the new version in order to continue getting universal credit.

What does a claimant commitment include?

The 'claimant commitment' is an agreement between you and the DWP. It sets out what you must do in return for receiving universal credit. This includes the 'work-related requirements' that are expected of you.

Your initial claimant commitment is usually drawn up by your work coach in a meeting after you claim. It includes the following information.

- Your work-related requirements.

- Details of what specific things you must do, and by when.

- By how much your universal credit will be reduced (or 'sanctioned'), and for how long, if you do not meet your requirements. There is more information about sanctions in Chapter 7.

- An instruction to report changes in your circumstances, and what happens if you do not do so.

- Details on your right to challenge a decision to give you a sanction. Chapter 8 has more information on challenging decisions you do not agree with.

If you must look for work, your claimant commitment also includes the kind of work you are available to do and the number of hours you are expected to spend searching for work.

EXAMPLE

The claimant commitment

Jenny is 32 and lives alone. She loses her job and claims universal credit. Her claimant commitment says that she is looking for work and will do anything she can to get work. It states that she must be available for full-time work (up to 48 hours a week) at any time. There is a section about the type of work that she is looking for initially, and what she must do every week to look for work. This includes that she must normally spend 35 hours a week searching for work, regular things she must do every week, and specific actions to be taken by the end of the month. It explains the sanctions that may apply if she does not meet one of these requirements. It states that she must report any relevant changes of circumstances, and the possible consequences if she does not do so. It explains her right to challenge a decision to sanction her universal credit if the DWP decides that she has not met these requirements.

How do you accept a claimant commitment?

What the law says

Accepting your claimant commitment

The DWP decides how you must accept your claimant commitment. You can be asked to accept it:

- online
- by telephone
- in person

If you do not accept your claimant commitment within the time allowed by the DWP after you claim, you do not usually get any universal credit until the day you finally accept it.

Regulation 15 The Universal Credit Regulations 2013

What happens if you do not accept a claimant commitment?

If you do not accept a claimant commitment, you are not entitled to universal credit at all. If you are part of a couple, you must both accept a commitment to be entitled.

You do not have to accept a claimant commitment if you do not have the capacity to do so – eg, because you have mental health problems and someone else (an 'appointee') is responsible for your universal credit claim. You can also be entitled to universal credit without agreeing a commitment in exceptional circumstances, such as if there is an emergency at home or if you are in hospital. You must accept a commitment as soon as you can do so, and should explain to the DWP why you could not accept it earlier.

If you do not agree to accept your claimant commitment, you may be offered a 'cooling-off period' (of no more than seven days) to think about this before a decision is made that you are not entitled to universal credit. If you are unhappy with the things you must do, you can ask for this to be reviewed before you accept your claimant commitment. However, unless the DWP decides that your request is reasonable, you are not entitled to any universal credit until the day you accept the commitment.

What CPAG says

Refusing to accept a claimant commitment

If you refuse to accept a claimant commitment and ask for it to be reviewed, you are only entitled to universal credit while it is being reviewed if the DWP accepts that your request is 'reasonable'. The universal credit regulations and guidance do not explain what this means. Unless your work coach suggests something that it is impossible for you to do, it is better to accept the claimant commitment and then ask for it to be reviewed after accepting it. This means that you are entitled to universal credit. Remember that if you do not meet your current work-related requirements while you are waiting for the review request to be decided, you may be given a sanction which reduces your universal credit.

Can you change your claimant commitment?

In practice, you may be able to discuss and agree changes to your claimant commitment with your work coach. However, the law gives the DWP the power to decide when and how your commitment is updated, even if you do not agree to this. Your commitment is updated regularly if you must look for work, as you agree specific actions with your work coach. You must agree to the updated version to remain entitled to universal credit.

Your commitment must be changed if there is a change in your circumstances that is relevant to your claim – eg, if you adopt a child or become entitled to a 'carer element' in your universal credit award.

If you are unhappy with what your claimant commitment currently says you must do, you can ask your work coach for this to be reviewed. You must continue to meet your work-related requirements while the commitment is being reviewed, otherwise you may be given a sanction which reduces your universal credit. There is more information about sanctions in Chapter 7.

2. What are you expected to do?

Your 'claimant commitment' lists the various things that you are expected to do in order to receive universal credit, all of which are designed to help you either move into work or increase the amount of work that you do. These are known as the 'work-related requirements'.

There are different levels of work-related requirements, depending on your circumstances. You may have to:

- look for work – this involves being available for work and searching for work
- prepare for work
- attend 'work-focused interviews'

Some people have to do all these things, while others do not have any work-related requirements at all.

Which work-related requirements do you have?

Group	Work-related requirements
You are a jobseeker, or you are not in one of the groups below. You are doing some work, but have low earnings, and are not in one of the groups below.	You have all the work-related requirements.
You have limited capabilty for work. You are a lone parent or the 'main carer' of a child aged two.	You must prepare for work and take part in work-focused interviews.
You are a lone parent or the main carer of a child aged one. You are a single foster carer of a child aged under 16, or the main foster carer in a couple. You have started caring for a friend's or relative's child within the past year.	You must take part in work-focused interviews.
You are caring for a severely disabled person. You have been assessed as having 'limited capability for work related activity'. You are heavily pregnant or have recently given birth. You are a lone parent or the main carer of a child under one. You are the main carer of a child you have adopted within the past year. You are over the age at which you could claim pension credit. You are a student getting a loan or certain grants. You are a young person in non-advanced education who is 'without parental support'. You have recently experienced domestic violence.	You have no work-related requirements.

There are four broad groups of people, each with different levels of work-related requirements. Use the table to identify the group you are likely to be in, and then look at the information in the rest of this chapter for more details. Remember that your partner may be in a different group to you.

If you already work, your work-related requirements may be reduced, depending on how much you earn.

If you do not meet your work-related requirements, your universal credit may be reduced ('sanctioned').

Who helps you to meet your work-related requirements?

When you claim universal credit, a 'work coach' in your local Jobcentre Plus office is normally responsible for making sure you meet your work-related requirements. The work coach does not make decisions about your entitlement to universal credit; s/he focuses on what your work-related requirements should be and whether you have met them or not.

In the longer term, the main person helping you to look or prepare for work may not be employed by the Department for Work and Pensions (DWP). You might be referred to the Work and Health Programme or another scheme provided by an organisation outside the DWP, including an unpaid work placement or a project focused on promoting employment in a particular sector.

Your claimant commitment should explain what you should do and when. Although an adviser employed by one of these schemes could be the person you see most often, the decisions about your universal credit entitlement – including whether it will be reduced (sanctioned) – are made by the DWP. The adviser may make recommendations to the DWP, particularly if you have not taken part in a scheme that your claimant commitment says you must attend.

If you are in a 'full service' area, your claimant commitment is mainly managed online using your online journal.

3. Who must look for work?

Unless you are in one of the groups who have fewer 'work-related requirements', you must look for work. The groups are listed in the table on page 74.

Looking for work usually involves two separate requirements:

- to be available for work
- to search for work

You must also take part in 'work-focused interviews' or prepare for work, if you are asked to do this.

What does being available for work mean?

Being available for work means that you must usually be willing and able to take up full-time work immediately. You are expected to accept a part-time job if you are offered one, unless you have a good reason for not doing so. You must normally take any job that pays at least the national minimum wage. You may be required to be available for work of up to 48 hours a week.

Usually, you must be available immediately for any job that is within 90 minutes' travel time (each way) of your home. You must also be immediately available for job interviews.

You may be able to restrict your work availability if:

- you have a good work history (for the first three months of your claim)
- you have a health problem or disability
- you are caring for a child or a disabled person

There are other limited special circumstances in which you may not have to be immediately available for work. These are explained later in this section.

Do you have a good work history?

If you have been in work recently, you may be able to restrict the type of work you are available to do for up to three months after you claim universal credit. This includes both the type of job and the level of pay. The decision to allow you to restrict the sort of work that you are looking for is at the discretion of your 'work coach', who must accept that you have a reasonable chance of getting this kind of work. This rule also applies if you already get universal credit and you have just lost a full-time or well-paid job.

Box A
Do you have a good work history?

Whether or not you can restrict the type of job you are looking for may depend on:

* the availability of the type of job you used to do
* your prospects of getting the kind of job you had previously
* the length of time you were employed in the same occupation
* how long it has been since your last job ended
* your skills and qualifications
* training you have done for the job

Do you have childcare responsibilities?
If you are a lone parent or the main carer of a child aged three or over but under 13, your availability for work is limited to be compatible with your child's school or nursery hours (including the time taken to travel to and from school or nursery).

If it is accepted as reasonable, you may not have to be available for work at all if you are the main carer of a child who has not yet started school or nursery, taking into account the availability of other childcare arrangements.

You may also be able to restrict your availability for work if you sometimes look after your child who lives with your ex-partner for part of the week, or if your child is 13 or over but you need to look after her/him, perhaps because s/he has additional support needs. If the Department for Work and Pensions (DWP) accepts that you have a reasonable prospect of finding work, you only have to be available for work that is considered compatible with your caring responsibilities. There is no set number of hours in this situation.

Do you have a disability or health problems?
If you have a disability or a health problem, but you do not meet the conditions for having 'limited capability for work' (there is more information about this in Chapter 5) or you are waiting for an assessment on whether you have limited capability for work, you may be able to restrict your availability for work. You must be available for the number of hours of work that is considered reasonable, taking account of your disability or health condition, but it does not matter if this restriction means that you do not have a reasonable chance of finding work.

If the DWP accepts that your condition has a substantial effect on your ability to carry out certain types of work, or work in a particular kind of place (eg, a dusty environment), you do not have to be available for this kind of work. You may have to provide evidence of how your condition or treatment limits the type, location or hours of work for which you are available.

If you are temporarily sick, you do not have to be available for work. You can only use this rule twice a year. You can 'self-certify' as sick for up to seven days, and provide a doctor's note for a further seven days after that. If you are sick for more than 14 days, you do not have to be available for work if the DWP accepts that this is reasonable. You may be asked to provide medical evidence.

If the DWP does not accept that you cannot be available for any work, try to limit the kind of work you are available for because of your health problems until you are assessed to see whether you have limited capability for work. Discuss what you are currently able to do with your work coach.

Do you care for a disabled person?
If you are caring for an ill or disabled person, but you do not meet the conditions for having no work-related requirements at all, you may be able to restrict your availability for work. Provided the DWP accepts that you have a reasonable chance of finding work, you only have to be available to work the number of hours that are considered compatible with your caring responsibilities. There is no set number of hours in this situation.

Do you have to be available for work immediately?

You are normally expected to start work or attend a job interview immediately. There are some exceptions to this, which are outlined below, but you must still be willing and able to start work or attend an interview at the end of the extra time you are given.

What the law says

Who may not need to be immediately available to attend an interview or start work

- If you are employed, you *must* be given 48 hours' notice to attend an interview, and you cannot be expected to take up a different job until the end of the notice period you must give in your current job.

- If you are doing voluntary work, you *may* be given up to 48 hours' notice to attend an interview and up to a week's notice to start paid work, if this is considered reasonable.

- If you are caring for a child or disabled person, you *may* be given up to 48 hours' notice to attend an interview and up to a month's notice to start work, if this is considered reasonable.

Regulation 96 The Universal Credit Regulations 2013

Are there any other special circumstances?

In certain specific circumstances, you cannot be required to be available for work, or to search for work. These include if your partner or child has recently died, your childcare has been disrupted, or if you are carrying out certain public duties. You should explain your situation to your work coach and ask for your 'claimant commitment' to be changed. However, you may still have to take part in work-focused interviews or prepare for work.

In other circumstances, provided your work coach agrees that it is reasonable, your work-related requirements can also be reduced. This applies if:

- you are doing training or other work preparation
- you are sick for longer than 14 days (you must provide evidence of this, if required)
- you are temporarily looking after a child
- you are dealing with a domestic emergency
- there is a temporary change in your circumstances

Even if one of the above circumstances applies, you must still be available for work, search for work and attend a job interview if your work coach thinks that this would be reasonable in your particular circumstances. If you do not do so, your universal credit may be reduced ('sanctioned'). If this happens, you can challenge this decision and argue that you had a good reason for failing to meet your requirements. Discuss your circumstances in advance with your work coach to try to avoid being sanctioned.

Do you already work?

If you are working, but you work fewer hours than your claimant commitment says you must, and your earnings are low, you are usually expected to be available for other jobs. This could be working more hours for your current employer, taking a second job or a different job with better pay.

You can be given a sanction if you do not take the job, unless your work coach agrees that you had a good reason for refusing it. To avoid this situation, make sure you discuss with your work coach the difficulties that taking a better paid job would cause you before refusing it – eg, if your current job allows you to work flexibly around your caring responsibilities, but the new one would not. If your universal credit is sanctioned, you can challenge the decision and argue that you had a good reason, but there is no guarantee that your challenge will be successful.

However, if you and your partner have more than a certain amount of earnings, you no longer need to be available for work or to search for work. This is called the 'earnings threshold'.

Your 'individual earnings threshold' is set at the monthly amount you would earn if you worked the number of hours that you must spend searching for work each week (normally 35 but may be lower if you have a physical or mental disability or caring responsibilities) and you were paid at the national minimum wage for your age. It is lower than this if you are an apprentice.

This same threshold applies if you are self-employed and you started your business within the last year. If you have been self-employed for over a year and it is your main occupation, you are treated as earning the amount of your individual earnings threshold (and so you have no work-related requirements), even if you actually earn less than this. This level of earnings is called the 'minimum income floor'. There is more information about how your earnings are calculated if you are self-employed in Chapter 5.

EXAMPLE

The earnings threshold

Cassie is a lone parent and has a nine-year-old son. She agrees with her work coach that her expected hours of work should be 25 a week to fit in with her son's normal school hours including the time it takes him to travel to and from school. Her earnings threshold is the national minimum wage multiplied by 25 and converted to a monthly amount.

If you live with a partner, in addition to your individual earnings threshold, you also have a 'joint earnings threshold'. This is the total amount you would earn if you both earned an amount equal to your individual thresholds. If your partner's circumstances mean that s/he does not have to look for work, s/he has a lower individual earnings threshold.

If your joint earnings are below the threshold, you are usually both expected to look for more work. However, if you already earn more than your individual threshold, but your partner does not, you do not have to look for more work, but your partner does.

If you live with a partner but must claim universal credit as a single person, your joint earnings threshold is calculated as if your partner was expected to work 35 hours a week.

EXAMPLE

The joint earnings threshold

Bob and Derek claim universal credit as a couple. They have no children, health problems or savings and they each have an individual earnings threshold of £1137.50. Their only other income is Derek's wages, which are £1,000 a month before tax and national insurance. Bob and Derek each get a letter telling them that they must look for more work.

Three months later, Bob finds a job paying £1,500 a month before tax and national insurance. The couple now earn more than their joint earnings threshold between them. This is twice the monthly amount someone on the national minimum wage working 35 hours a week would earn. Because of this, neither of them have any work-related requirements.

If your earnings vary, your average monthly earnings, before deducting any tax or national insurance contributions, are used. If you have a normal cycle of work, your earnings are averaged over one cycle. If not, your earnings are normally averaged over three months.

What does searching for work mean?

You must usually do anything that is reasonable to help you find work, as well as any specific actions in your claimant commitment.

You must usually spend 35 hours a week searching for work, unless you can restrict the number of hours.

If you can restrict your work availability to less than 35 hours a week because of your childcare or caring responsibilities, or because you have a physical or mental disability, you are only expected to spend the number of hours you must be available to work on your work search. The situations in which you can restrict your availability for work are explained in more detail on pages 77 and 78.

Box B
Searching for work

Work search may include spending time on specific activities such as:

- looking for jobs online
- applying for particular jobs
- maintaining an online profile
- registering with an employment agency
- cold-calling employers
- seeking references

The action you take must give you the best chance of finding a job. You can also be asked to spend time preparing for work.

When you first claim universal credit you are likely to be asked to create an account on the Universal Jobmatch website, update your CV and create an email address, if you have not already done all of these things.

EXAMPLE

Searching for work

Samantha has been claiming universal credit and looking for work for over four months. During this time she has registered with several employment agencies, and applied for specific jobs discussed with her work coach. At a meeting to discuss Samantha's work-related requirements, her work coach decides that she needs to do a training course to make her skills more attractive to employers.

Although this is a work preparation requirement, Samantha can be asked to do this as well. Her work coach temporarily changes her claimant commitment to state that she can deduct the hours she spends on the training course from the time she must spend searching for work each week.

Regular work search activities are likely to include checking the Universal Jobmatch website and employment agency websites, contacting potential employers and applying for any specific jobs identified by your work coach.

Keep as much evidence of what you have done to look for work as you can. The more evidence you have, the more likely the DWP will accept that you have been searching for work (and you will not be sanctioned for failing to do so).

Do you already work or volunteer?
If you already have a job, the hours you spend at work should be deducted from the time you must spend searching for work each week.

If you are doing voluntary work, the number of hours that you must spend searching for work can also be reduced, provided your work coach accepts that your volunteering gives you the best chance of finding paid work. However, the number of hours that you can spend volunteering is limited to half the number of hours you are expected to spend searching for work.

You can also deduct the time it takes to travel to and from work.

In any of the above circumstances, the DWP must agree that you can reduce your hours of work search.

EXAMPLE

Work search if you already have a job

Dylan is single and has no caring responsibilities or health problems, so he must search for work for 35 hours a week. He gets a job that is one day a week, working six hours. He must drive one hour each way to get to and from work. Although he must still be available for full-time work, he now only needs to look for more work for 27 hours a week, as his work coach agrees that it is reasonable for him to deduct the eight hours that he spends working and travelling.

Have you done everything that is reasonable to search for work?
If your work coach agrees that you have done everything that could reasonably be expected of you in a particular week, you have met your work search requirement, even if you spent less time searching for work than your claimant commitment says. This may also be the case if you have had a temporary change in your circumstances, such as moving house, a child being excluded from school or an emergency at home, which has meant that you have been unable to spend as long as you should have searching for work.

What CPAG says

Hours of work search

The decision to accept a reduced number of hours of work search as reasonable is at the discretion of your work coach. Discuss this in advance with her/him and try to agree that you will look for work for a reduced number of hours. Remember that if this is not agreed, you may be sanctioned if you do not stick to the hours of work search in your claimant commitment.

4. Who must prepare for work?

Some people are not expected to look for work, but must prepare for a future return to work. This applies to you if you have significant health problems or disabilities, or if you are a lone parent or the main carer of a child aged two. You must also take part in 'work-focused interviews' if asked to do so.

Do you already work?

If you already work but your earnings are low, you may still be required to prepare for work.

However, if you must prepare for work but do not also have to look for work and your earnings are over a certain amount, you do not have any 'work-related requirements' at all. Your monthly earnings, before deducting tax and national insurance contributions, must be over the amount you would earn if you worked 16 hours a week at the national minimum wage for someone your age. This is known as the 'earnings threshold'.

What the law says

Work preparation

Work preparation can include spending a set amount of time on activities including:
- having a skills assessment
- attending a health and work conversation
- improving your personal presentation
- doing training
- participating in a government employment programme
- doing work experience or unpaid work placements
- developing your own business plan

Other activities may be added to the list if your work coach thinks it is necessary.

Section 16 Welfare Reform Act 2012

If your earnings vary, your average monthly earnings, before deducting any tax or national insurance contributions, are used. If you have a normal cycle of work, your earnings are averaged over one cycle. If not, your earnings are normally averaged over three months.

What do you *not* have to do?

If you must prepare for work, you do not have to search for, apply for or take a job. These are different 'work-related requirements'. However, you could be expected to do work experience or a work placement with an employer. If you are caring for a disabled person or a young child, you may need to explain this to your 'work coach' and ask to be given only 'work preparation' activities that are compatible with your caring responsibilities. However, there is no right to this, and if you do not comply with the requirement, your universal credit may be reduced ('sanctioned').

Are you ill or disabled?

If you are ill or disabled and currently unfit for work, tell the Department for Work and Pensions. You must attend an assessment to decide whether your health or disability is a serious barrier to work. This is called the 'limited capability for work' test. It is also used to decide whether you qualify for employment and support allowance. There is more information about this in Chapter 5.

If you are assessed as having limited capability for work, you must prepare for work or take part in work-focused interviews if asked to do so. If you are waiting to be assessed, or it is decided that you do not have limited capability for work and you have appealed against this decision, you must normally look for work.

EXAMPLE

Preparing for work

Thomas has bipolar disorder, which affects his ability to work. He is assessed as having limited capability for work, but must prepare for work. Thomas used to work in an office years ago, but is worried that his knowledge of computing will not be good enough to get a similar job when he is able to return to work.

He attends a work-focused interview and agrees that he will attend a two-month computing course to update his skills. His work coach agrees to help him look for a one-week work placement after the course ends, so he can see how well he copes with being at work. A separate assessment of how his mental health will affect his ability to manage a job may also be arranged.

Are you caring for a young child?

If you are a lone parent or the main carer of a child who is two, you must prepare for work. You must also take part in work-focused interviews if asked to do so.

5. Who must take part in work-focused interviews?

If your circumstances are a significant barrier to your being able to work full time, you may only have to take part in 'work-focused interviews'. You have no other 'work-related requirements' as a condition of getting universal credit. You may be in this group if you look after a child who is one, or vulnerable children, or if you are a foster carer.

Do you already work?

If you already work but your earnings are low, you may still be required to take part in work-focused interviews.

However, if you are in one of the groups of people who must only take part in work-focused interviews, and your earnings are over a certain amount, you do not have any work-related requirements at all. Your monthly earnings before deducting tax and national insurance contributions must be over the amount you would earn if you worked 16 hours a week at the national minimum wage for someone your age. This is known as the 'earnings threshold'.

If your earnings vary, your average monthly earnings, before deducting any tax or national insurance contributions, are used. If you have a normal cycle of work, your earnings are averaged over one cycle. If not, your earnings are normally averaged over three months.

What happens at a work-focused interview?

The purpose of a work-focused interview is to discuss how you can remain in or obtain work, including getting more work if you work already.

Box C
What is discussed at a work-focused interview?

Subjects likely to be discussed include:

- any work that you currently do, including self-employment
- how you can stay in work or increase your earnings
- your qualifications and training
- any medical condition or disability you have which may be a barrier to working
- your caring or childcare responsibilities and how they affect your ability to work
- potential work and training opportunities for the future
- accessing help and support to assist you to work

Are you caring for a young child?

If you are a lone parent or the main carer of a child who is one year old, you must take part in work-focused interviews.

EXAMPLE

Work-focused interviews

Anwar is the main carer for his daughter Aisha. She is one year old and is looked after by Anwar's mother every weekday morning. Anwar drops her off and picks her up, but he is able to work two hours a day during the time Aisha is with her grandmother. He thinks that he might be able to work more hours once Aisha turns three and he qualifies for a free childcare place. He must take part in work-focused interviews when asked to do so.

Even if Anwar's work coach thinks that he needs to do more to prepare for working more hours in the future, this cannot be added to his claimant commitment until Aisha turns two.

Are you a foster carer?

There are special rules for registered foster carers who have a child placed with them. If you are looking after a friend's or relative's child who is 'looked after' by the local authority, you may count as a foster carer under these rules. If you are a single foster carer or the main carer in a couple, you must take part in work-focused interviews, but have no other work-related requirements, from your foster child's first birthday until s/he turns 16.

Your partner normally has the work-related requirements that are appropriate for her/him.

You must attend work-focused interviews, but have no other work-related requirements, if you are the main carer of a foster child aged 16 to 19 who has extra care needs, or if your partner is the main carer but you both need to care for your foster child because of the level of her/his care needs. The Department for Work and Pensions must accept that it is reasonable for you not to have to look for work, even for a limited number of hours a week.

If you are between fostering placements, you do not have any additional work-related requirements for the first eight weeks after your last placement ended, provided you intend to continue fostering.

Are you looking after a child of a friend or relative?

If you are the main carer of a child of any age whose parents are dead or unable to look after her/him, you must take part in work-focused interviews (but you have no other work-related requirements) during the first year after you become the child's main carer.

If the child in these circumstances is being 'looked after' by the local authority, you may instead count as a foster carer and have no other work-related requirements until s/he turns 16.

6. Who has no work-related requirements?

In certain circumstances, you cannot be asked to meet any 'work-related requirements' to get universal credit. However, you must still agree a 'claimant commitment' to get universal credit.

Are you caring for a severely disabled person?

You have no work-related requirements if you get a 'carer element' in your universal credit. You get this if you care for a severely disabled person for at least 35 hours a week, and no one else gets a carer element for caring for the same person. You do not count as a carer under these rules if you are working as a paid carer, or if you are in full-time education.

The definition of who is a 'severely disabled person' is linked to the rate of disability living allowance, personal independence payment or attendance allowance received by the person you care for.

If you do not qualify for the carer element – perhaps because someone else gets it for looking after the same severely disabled person – but you spend 35 hours or more a week caring, you may still not have any work-related requirements. However, this decision is at the discretion of the Department for Work and Pensions (DWP). It must accept that it would be unreasonable for you to look for any work at all, even for a limited number of hours.

There is more information about universal credit and carers in Chapter 9.

Are you over pension age?

If you are over the age at which you cannot claim universal credit as a single person, but you must claim universal credit because you live with a younger partner, you have no work-related requirements. Your partner may have work-related requirements. There is more information about the age limits for claiming universal credit in Chapter 3, and more information about older people and universal credit in Chapter 9.

Are you pregnant or caring for a child under one?

If you are pregnant and your baby is due in 11 weeks or less, or you gave birth within the last 15 weeks, you have no work-related requirements.

In addition, if you are either a lone parent or the 'main carer' in a couple and have a child aged under one included as part of your family in your universal credit award or you are fostering a child under one, you have no work-related requirements. You and your partner can decide who is the main carer. Only one of you can be the main carer, even if you have more than one child.

You can change who the main carer is once a year, or more frequently than this if the DWP accepts that there has been a relevant change in your household circumstances.

EXAMPLE

The main carer

Luis and Patricia have a joint claim for universal credit. Neither of them work. When their son Pablo is born (their first child), they decide to nominate Patricia as the main carer. She has no work-related requirements, and Luis is looking for work. Patricia is offered a job when Pablo is six months old. She cannot take the job unless there is someone else to look after Pablo, so the couple nominate Luis as the main carer instead. Luis no longer has to look for work. Patricia is able to take the job while Luis looks after Pablo.

Because the rule about having recently given birth is separate from the rule about being the main carer of your children, a couple can nominate the father of a new baby as the main carer of all their children, so he can help with childcare around the time of the birth without having to worry about meeting any work-related requirements.

However, the decision to change the main carer more than once in a year is at the discretion of the DWP. You should therefore discuss your plans with your work coach in advance. If your work-related requirements are not reduced, you should continue to meet them and ask for your claimant commitment to be reviewed, as otherwise your universal credit may be reduced ('sanctioned').

Have you recently adopted a child?

If you are the main carer of a child with whom you have been matched for adoption, you have no work-related requirements for one year after the child is placed with you. If you want, you can choose that this period starts up to two weeks before the child is placed with you. These rules do not apply if you were a foster parent or close relative of the child before adopting her/him.

Are you severely ill or disabled?

If you have serious health problems or disabilities, and are assessed by the DWP as having 'limited capability for work-related activity', you get an additional 'element' included in your universal credit award. You also have no work-related requirements.

There is more information about the test of limited capability for work-related activity in Chapter 5.

Are you a student?

If you are a full-time student and you receive a grant or loan that is counted as income for universal credit, you have no work-related requirements. Remember that most students are not eligible to claim universal credit at all. This is explained in Chapter 3.

This rule applies to you during the months in which your student income is taken into account in calculating your universal credit award, so you may still have some work-related requirements during the long summer vacation.

You also do not have any work-related requirements if you are a young student in non-advanced education and you can claim universal credit because you do not get any support from your parents.

Have you recently experienced domestic violence?

Even if you would normally have to meet some (or all) of the work-related requirements, you do not have to do so for 13 weeks if you have experienced domestic violence. You must no longer live with the perpetrator and you must tell the DWP within six months of the violence. Within one month of notifying the DWP, you must provide evidence that the abuse is likely to have occurred. This must be from one of a list of professionals, including a police officer or social worker.

You can only be exempted from your work-related requirements once in any one-year period.

If you are the main carer of a child and would normally have to look for work at the end of this 13-week period, you cannot be required to look for work for a further 13 weeks. However, you can be required to take part in 'work-focused interviews' or prepare for work.

The definition of 'domestic violence' includes controlling or coercive behaviour or actual or threatened physical, financial, psychological, emotional or sexual abuse, where the perpetrator was either your partner or certain other relatives.

Further information

On www.gov.uk there is *Advice for Decision Making*, produced by the Department for Work and Pensions for its own staff. Chapters J1 to J3 explain the claimant commitment and work-related requirements.
There is more information on the work-related requirements that apply to universal credit in CPAG's *Welfare Benefits and Tax Credits Handbook*.

Chapter 7
Sanctions and fines

This chapter covers:

1. When can your universal credit be sanctioned?

2. When is your universal credit not sanctioned?

3. How much is a sanction and how long does it last?

4. When can you get a hardship payment?

5. When can you be fined?

6. What happens to your universal credit after a benefit offence?

What you need to know

- If you do not meet your 'work-related requirements', the amount of your universal credit can be reduced. This is called being 'sanctioned'. The sanction can last indefinitely or for a set period. You should not be given a sanction if you have a good reason for not meeting a requirement.

- If you cannot meet your essential needs because of a sanction, you may be able to get a 'hardship payment'. This is a loan, which you may have to repay.

- If you are overpaid universal credit because you did not provide information or you gave incorrect information, you may be given a 'civil penalty'.

- If you give false information or act dishonestly in relation to your claim and it is serious enough for there to be grounds to prosecute you for fraud, you may be able to accept a fine instead of being prosecuted. If you accept a fine, your universal credit is also sanctioned.

1. When can your universal credit be sanctioned?

If you do not meet your 'work-related requirements' in your 'claimant commitment', your universal credit can be reduced. This is called being 'sanctioned'. The amount of the sanction and how long it lasts depends on whether or not you must look for work as part of your work-related requirements and the reason for the sanction. A sanction should not be imposed if you had a 'good reason' for acting as you did.

Do you have to look for work?

If you have to look for work as a condition of getting universal credit, you can be sanctioned if, for example, you do not do something that is set out in your claimant commitment. There are three levels of sanctions.

You can be given a **high-level** sanction if:

- you do not apply for a particular job
- you do not take up a job offer
- you do not take up a work placement
- you give up a job or lose pay voluntarily or because of misconduct

You can be given a **medium-level** sanction if:

- you are not available to start work immediately
- you are not doing enough to find work

You can be given a **low-level** sanction if:

- you do not undertake any of your other work-related requirements, such as updating your CV
- you do not report a change of circumstances, provide information or attend an interview relevant to your work-related requirements

EXAMPLES

Sanctions if you must look for work

Mandy lives alone and has no health problems. She gives up her job because she finds it boring and claims universal credit. The Department for Work and Pensions (DWP) does not accept that Mandy had a good reason for leaving her job and decides that her universal credit will be sanctioned for 91 days.

Eric and Freya claim universal credit as a couple and are both looking for work. Freya misses an interview for a course which her 'work coach' thinks she should attend. She receives a low-level sanction because she failed to attend an interview relevant to her work-related activity.

Do you *not* have to look for work?

Even if you do not have to look for work, your universal credit can be sanctioned if you do not do something that is set out in your claimant commitment. There are two levels of sanctions.

You can be given a **low-level** sanction if you are expected to prepare for work and, for instance:

- you do not take up a work placement you are told to do
- you do not undertake any of the activities that you are required to do to prepare for work
- you do not take part in an interview to discuss your work-related requirements
- you do not report a change in your circumstances that affects your work-related requirements

You can be given a **lowest level** sanction if you are expected to attend 'work-focused interviews' (but have no other work-related requirements) and, for instance:

- you do not attend or participate in a work-focused interview
- you do not report a change of circumstances relevant to your work-related requirements
- you do not attend an interview relevant to your work-related requirements

EXAMPLE

Sanctions if you do not have to look for work

Joachim is unable to work because of his mental health problems, but he is expected to prepare for work, including taking up work placements. His work coach finds him a work placement that she thinks is suitable. On the day the placement begins, Joachim forgets to set his alarm and misses the introductory session. He is given a low-level sanction.

2. When is your universal credit not sanctioned?

You can take steps to reduce the chances of your universal credit being 'sanctioned'. In some situations, the Department for Work and Pensions (DWP) should not give you a sanction.

You can avoid a sanction by understanding what is expected of you as a condition of your getting universal credit. This should be set out in your 'claimant commitment'. There is more information on this in Chapter 6.

Make sure that the DWP understands your current circumstances, so that you are only expected to undertake the relevant 'work-related requirements' and your claimant commitment matches these. If you do the things that are in your claimant commitment, you should not be given a sanction.

Avoiding sanctions

• Remember, you are not expected to meet all the possible work-related requirements in certain circumstances – eg, if you are caring for a young child or a severely disabled person.

• In some circumstances, you may be able to limit the number of hours you are expected to work or you may not need to be available for work immediately – eg, if you have a child under 13 in school or if you already have a part-time job.

• If you are finding it hard to do everything in your claimant commitment or you think a condition is unreasonable, ask your 'work coach' to review it.

• Keep a written record of everything you do to look or prepare for work and take it to any interviews or when you 'sign on', or write it in your online journal.

• If your circumstances change, tell your work coach immediately, as your claimant commitment may also need to change. If you are in a 'full service' area, you can report changes of circumstances using your online journal.

• Some or all of the conditions in your claimant commitment must be suspended in certain circumstances – eg, if you are bereaved or if you are having some types of medical treatment. Inform your work coach as soon as possible.

• If you are expected to attend an interview or a course or placement, you should receive notification and details in advance. If you have not, you should not be given a sanction for not participating.

• Try to stick to your claimant commitment, but if you have a 'good reason' for not keeping to it, let your work coach know as soon as possible. If you are in a 'full service' area, you can do this using your online journal.

EXAMPLE

Avoiding a sanction

Marshall has recently started claiming universal credit after being made redundant. His claimant commitment says that he is expected to be available for, and search for, work for 35 hours a week. However, he has responsibility for his nine-year-old daughter and can only be available for work and look for work while she is at school. He is struggling to show that he is meeting all his work-related requirements. When he goes to sign on he talks to his work coach, who agrees that it is reasonable for him to restrict the number of hours he is expected to work. His claimant commitment is changed to say that he must search for work for 20 hours a week.

Do you have a good reason?

In most cases, if you can show that you had a good reason for not meeting a requirement, your universal credit is not reduced – ie, you are not sanctioned.

What 'good reason' means is not defined in the rules, but there is guidance about the kinds of circumstances that can be taken into account. As well as these general factors, there may be other specific circumstances in your case. For example, you may have a good reason not to apply for a job if the cost of your childcare or travel is an unreasonably high proportion of the pay.

The DWP should consider all your circumstances and then decide whether or not you have a good reason. When making this decision, it normally uses information from your work coach, as s/he may have asked for a decision on whether you should be given a sanction. Make sure you give your own explanation too.

Box A
What is a good reason?

Examples of what may be relevant when deciding whether or not you have a good reason include if:

- there is a domestic emergency
- you have a mental health condition
- you have a disability
- you have learning disabilities
- you are homeless
- you have experienced domestic violence
- you have experienced bullying or harassment
- you have caring responsibilities
- you are offered a zero-hour contract which excludes you from taking other work

EXAMPLE

Good reason

Terry is made redundant after doing the same job for 15 years. At an interview just after he claims universal credit, his work coach suggests that he should apply for a similar job with a different employer, which is being advertised on the Universal Jobmatch website. Terry agrees to do this.

Before applying, Terry contacts the employer for more details. The job is not based at the main office, which means Terry would be working a long way from home. He would have to travel for about two hours to get to work, and the train and bus fares would cost him almost half of the salary on offer. Terry explains this to his work coach and it is accepted that he has a good reason for not applying for the job.

Have you left work or lost earnings voluntarily or because of misconduct?

If you leave your job or change your hours so that you lose earnings, your universal credit may be sanctioned. Your benefit should only be sanctioned if you have either done this voluntarily without a good reason or it has happened because of your misconduct.

The words 'voluntarily' and 'misconduct' are not defined in any special way. Box B lists some issues to bear in mind.

Box B
What is misconduct?

- Being careless or negligent, or refusing to do something without a good reason might be misconduct if it is serious enough. Being dismissed for poor performance is not necessarily misconduct.

- Misconduct must normally be connected with your employment in some way, although it does not necessarily need to happen while you are working.

- Dishonesty is clearly misconduct if it means that your employer does not trust you and dismisses you because of this.

- Being persistently late or being off sick without explaining the situation to your employer might be misconduct.

- If you resign to avoid being dismissed, this can count as misconduct.

- If your employer says you were dismissed because of misconduct, but is really just reducing staff numbers, this should not count as misconduct.

You should not be given a sanction if:

- you are made redundant or take voluntary redundancy
- you leave or lose pay as a member of the armed forces, even if you left voluntarily

- you have been laid off or put on short-time working by your employer
- you leave a job or lose pay while still in a trial period
- you are involved in a trade dispute
- you leave a job or lose pay, but your weekly earnings do not fall below the 'earnings threshold' in your claimant commitment

3. How much is a sanction and how long does it last?

If you are given a 'sanction', the most your universal credit can be reduced by is an amount equal to the adult 'standard allowance' that applies to you. If you are claiming as a couple and only one of you receives a sanction, the maximum reduction is half of your standard allowance as a couple.

You can be sanctioned for an indefinite period or a set number of days. A sanction starts from the beginning of the monthly 'assessment period' in which it is given.

How much is a sanction?

As the length of a sanction is a particular number of days, the amount of the sanction is also worked out on a daily basis. The amount depends on whether you are single or a couple, and whether you are over or under 25.

For each day in the sanction period, the amount that applies to you is deducted from your universal credit award.

The lower rate applies if:

- you are given a 'lowest level' sanction
- you are aged 16 or 17

Daily rate of sanction, 2017/18

	Usual rate £ per day	Lower rate £ per day
Single		
Under 25	8.20	3.30
25 or over	10.40	4.10
Couple (per person sanctioned)		
Both under 25	6.40	2.50
One 25 or over	8.20	3.20

EXAMPLE

The amount of a sanction

Duncan is 43, single and unemployed. His 'work coach' notifies him of a job vacancy, but Duncan does not apply for it because his mother is taken into hospital that day. He is given a sanction for 91 days. The sanction is applied for the whole of his monthly assessment periods for April, May and June.

His usual universal credit award is £617.82 a month, made up of £317.82 standard allowance and £300 housing costs. The sanction is £312 in April and June (30 days x £10.40) and £317.82 for May (31 days x £10.40, limited to the amount of his standard allowance). He gets paid about £300 a month for those three months, just enough to cover his rent, but not enough for bills or food. Duncan does three things.

- He contacts his work coach to explain his reasons for not applying for the vacancy.

- He asks an advice centre for help challenging the sanction.

- He applies for a 'hardship payment'.

The amount of the sanction may be the same as, or more than, the amount of your universal credit award. If this is the case, you are paid no universal credit for the period of the sanction.

If your universal credit is sanctioned, you may find that you are left without enough money to pay for essential items, such as food and bills. If this is the case, you can apply for a hardship payment. There is more information about hardship payments on page 107.

How long does a sanction last?

Length of sanctions

Level of sanction	Length of sanction		
	First failure	*Second failure within a year*	*Third failure within a year*
High level – eg, you failed to apply for a job	91 days	182 days	1,095 days
Medium level – eg, you failed to take all reasonable action to get work	28 days	91 days	91 days
Low level – eg, you failed to take particular action to prepare for work	Until you comply plus seven days after that	Until you comply plus 14 days after that	Until you comply plus 28 days after that
Lowest level – eg, you failed to attend a work-focused interview	Until you comply	Until you comply	Until you comply

The number of days a sanction lasts depends on the level of sanction and whether you have been sanctioned before. Sometimes the sanction lasts until you comply with the work-related requirement, rather than for a set period.

Shorter sanction periods apply to 16/17-year-olds.

EXAMPLE

Length of a sanction

Jerry has been assessed as having 'limited capability for work'. He is required to prepare for work. He gets a low-level sanction because he did not attend a training course his work coach found for him and he did not have a good reason for failing to attend. This is the first time Jerry has been sanctioned.

Jerry and his work coach agree that if he attends a different course, he will be treated as having met the original requirement and his sanction will end a week after he starts the course.

If you are already being sanctioned and you get another sanction, the new sanction starts when the current one ends. This means getting sanctioned again results in a longer sanction period rather than a higher daily rate of sanction. However, you cannot have more than a total of 1,095 days of sanctions applied to you at any one time.

What happens if your circumstances change?

The sanction period continues, even if your universal credit award ends. If you reclaim universal credit before the sanction period ends, the sanction continues for the remainder of the period.

If, since the start of your last sanction, you are in work for 26 weeks and earning above a certain amount, any remaining sanctions on your universal credit award are written off.

Weeks in different jobs with gaps in between can count towards the 26 weeks.

The daily amount of a sanction is reduced to zero (ie, you get your full universal credit entitlement) if you become unwell and you are assessed as having 'limited capability for work-related activity' and so you have no work-related requirements. There is more information about this assessment in Chapter 5. The sanction period continues, so that if your health improves before the sanction period ends, the sanction can start again.

EXAMPLE

Continuation of a sanction

Belle receives a high-level sanction of 182 days because she left her job voluntarily and then did not take up an offer of a suitable new job within a year. Eight weeks (56 days) after the start of the sanction period, she gets a new job. Her earnings mean that she no longer qualifies for universal credit, so her award stops. However, Belle's new job ends after three months (92 days) as the company goes into administration, and she reclaims universal credit immediately. Her new award of universal credit continues to be sanctioned until 182 days after the sanction period first started.

4. When can you get a hardship payment?

If the amount of your universal credit is reduced because of a 'sanction', you may be able to get a 'hardship payment'. These are loans and are usually recovered from your universal credit.

To get a hardship payment, you must be unable to meet your immediate essential needs as a result of your benefit being sanctioned. These are your:

- accommodation
- heating
- food
- hygiene

You should be able to meet the immediate needs of yourself, your partner and your children. If you cannot, you may get a hardship payment.

If you are 16 or 17, or you are sanctioned at the lower or nil rate, you cannot get a hardship payment. This is because the sanction has not reduced your universal credit by the full 'standard allowance'.

To get a hardship payment, you must make an application and provide any required information. You must also continue to meet your 'work-related requirements'. It is important that you explain your circumstances when you apply for a hardship payment. The Department for Work and Pensions (DWP) is more likely to accept that you need one if, for example, you have children or caring responsibilities, or if you are ill or pregnant. You can appeal if you are refused a hardship payment.

You may need to show that you have tried other sources of support to meet your essential needs, such as help from relatives. You may also have to show that you have tried to stop spending on anything other than your essential needs.

How much are hardship payments and how long do they last?

Hardship payments are paid at 60 per cent of the amount by which your universal credit has been reduced. For example, if you are a single person over 25 and your universal credit is sanctioned for seven days so that your monthly payment is reduced by £72.80, the maximum hardship payment you can get before your next normal universal credit payment is due is £43.68.

Usually a hardship payment is paid until your next universal credit payment is due. You must then apply again the following month – ie, for each new monthly 'assessment period'.

When do you repay a hardship payment?

Once the sanction period is over, you normally start to pay back the hardship payment. This is usually by having your universal credit award reduced until the payment is repaid, in the same way as if you were paying back an overpayment of universal credit. There is more information about repaying overpayments in Chapter 8.

However, sometimes you do not need to pay it back at all or for a period.

- You do not repay a hardship payment while you are working and earning above a certain amount.

- If you are in work and earning above a certain amount for 26 weeks, any hardship payment you have not yet repaid is written off completely.

EXAMPLE

Hardship payments

Anita and Tony have two children, aged six and eight. Tony has just resigned from his job and the couple have claimed universal credit. Tony is given a sanction for leaving his job without a good reason. He is 'signing on' and looking for work. Anita is pregnant and unwell because of complications in her pregnancy. The couple have no other income. They explain their circumstances to the DWP and provide evidence to show that they cannot meet their essential needs, have no non-essential expenditure and have not been able to get help from other members of their family. The DWP decides that they can get a hardship payment of universal credit.

Tony finds a new job. As it pays enough, the recovery of their hardship payments is suspended and, after 26 weeks, they are written off.

Tony can also appeal against the decision to sanction their universal credit. He could argue that his wife's pregnancy and illness, together with the needs of their children, were good reasons for leaving his job (if this was why he stopped work).

5. When can you be fined?

There are two types of fines that you can receive while you are getting universal credit.

- You can be given a 'civil penalty' if you are overpaid universal credit because of something that you have done.

- You can be given a 'penalty as an alternative to prosecution' if the Department for Work and Pensions (DWP) thinks there may be grounds to prosecute you for fraud.

Get advice immediately if you are being prosecuted for benefit fraud, have been offered a fine to avoid the possibility of being prosecuted, or have been asked to attend a formal interview.

When can you be given a civil penalty?

You can be given a civil penalty of £50 if you have been overpaid universal credit by at least £65.01. The overpayment must have occurred because:

- you negligently made an incorrect statement
- you negligently provided incorrect information or evidence
- you failed to report a relevant change of circumstances 'without a reasonable excuse'

In the first two cases, you are not given a penalty if you have taken 'reasonable steps' to correct your error.

The DWP has discretion about when to fine you and can decide whether you have been 'negligent' or have taken 'reasonable steps' to correct an error. For example, you might not be fined, even if you have been overpaid, if you have a mental health problem and you did not understand what you were doing.

You can only be given a civil penalty if you have not been charged with an offence or given a fine as an alternative to being prosecuted in connection with the same overpayment.

If you are given a civil penalty but you do not think you were negligent, or you think you had a reasonable excuse, or the overpayment was not worked out correctly, you may be able to appeal against the decision.

EXAMPLE

Civil penalty

Nigel works part time. His daughter Clara attends nursery while he works and he receives help towards the costs of childcare in his universal credit. Nigel decides that he wants to spend more time with Clara, reorganises his work and reduces her childcare by a few hours a week. He mistakenly reports the wrong amount of childcare costs for two months. The DWP decides that Nigel has been negligent, but that the situation is not sufficiently serious to prosecute him for fraud. Nigel's universal credit award is amended, an overpayment of £180 is calculated and a £50 penalty is added to it.

Nigel can appeal against the decision to add a penalty to his overpayment if he has a reasonable excuse for not informing the DWP earlier.

A fine cannot be imposed on your partner if s/he was unaware of your negligence, or if s/he has a reasonable excuse for not providing the information needed.

When can you be given a penalty instead of being prosecuted?

If the DWP thinks there are grounds for prosecuting you for a benefit fraud offence, you may be offered a penalty instead. If you accept this fine, you cannot be prosecuted for the same offence.

You have 14 days after accepting the fine to change your mind and withdraw your acceptance. If you withdraw your acceptance, the DWP must refund any of the fine you have already paid, but may decide to prosecute you instead.

If you accept a penalty as an alternative to being prosecuted, the amount you are fined (in 2017/18) is:

- £350 if there has been no overpayment
- 50 per cent of the overpayment, subject to a minimum of £350 and a maximum of £5,000

It may be difficult to decide what to do. On the one hand, if you accept the fine, you avoid prosecution. On the other hand, you must pay the fine and your universal credit will be sanctioned for a period. Always get independent advice to help you decide.

EXAMPLE

Penalty instead of prosecution

Aaron claims universal credit for himself and his two children. Before any payment is made, his claim is turned down, as the DWP believes the children live with his ex-wife Maria, who already gets universal credit for them. Aaron has not provided any evidence of when the children stay with him. Although no overpayment has been made to Aaron, the DWP believes that he deliberately claimed for the children dishonestly in order to get more benefit, and so he could be prosecuted for fraud. Rather than start proceedings, Aaron is offered the alternative of paying a £350 fine. He should get advice before accepting this.

Depending on the children's living arrangements, Aaron may also be able to argue that he can claim for the children.

To be convicted, the DWP must prove that Aaron knew he was not entitled to amounts of universal credit for them and was acting dishonestly.

How do you pay a fine?

A fine is recoverable from you in the same way as an overpayment. There is more information about overpayments and how they are recovered in Chapter 8.

If you have a joint universal credit claim, the fine is recovered from your joint award. It may also be recovered by other methods (eg, deductions from other benefits or from earnings) from you or from your partner.

If a fine is being recovered from you and the decision that you have been overpaid is later changed (eg, if your appeal against the decision is successful), the DWP must refund any amount of the fine that you have already paid.

6. What happens to your universal credit after a benefit offence?

If you are convicted of a benefit offence or you accept a fine to avoid possible prosecution, your universal credit entitlement is also 'sanctioned' for a set period of time. This usually means that you are paid less benefit but, in some cases, it can mean losing entitlement altogether. You can apply for a 'hardship payment'.

The sanction lasts for four weeks if you accept a penalty instead of prosecution. If you are prosecuted and convicted and it is your first offence, the sanction usually lasts for 13 weeks. If you are convicted again for another benefit offence, the sanction is longer.

EXAMPLE

Sanction for a benefit offence

Connor accepts a fine of 50 per cent of the amount of an overpayment of universal credit as an alternative to being prosecuted, after it was found that he had not declared the casual work he had been doing. As well as the fine, he is given a sanction for four weeks.

Further information

The official guidance about sanctions and hardship payments is in the DWP's *Advice for Decision Making* at www.gov.uk/government/publications/advice-for-decision-making-staff-guide.
There is also more information about fraud and penalties in CPAG's *Welfare Benefits and Tax Credits Handbook*.

Chapter 8
Dealing with universal credit problems

This chapter covers:

1. What can you do if there is a problem with your universal credit?

2. What happens if you are overpaid?

3. Do you disagree with a decision?

4. How do you complain?

What you need to know

- If you are overpaid universal credit, the Department for Work and Pensions (DWP) can recover it, even if the overpayment was caused by its own mistake.

- The DWP has the discretion not to recover an overpayment, but is only likely to do this in exceptional circumstances.

- If the DWP decides to recover an overpayment, you cannot appeal against this. However, you may be able to challenge the decision in other ways.

- The DWP usually recovers an overpayment from your ongoing award of universal credit, but may recover it in other ways, including from your earnings.

- If you are unhappy about most decisions about your universal credit, you can appeal to an independent tribunal. Before you do so, you must ask the DWP to consider revising the decision.

- If you cannot appeal, you can still complain about the way your universal claim has been handled.

1. What can you do if there is a problem with your universal credit?

Various problems can arise with your universal credit award or payment. What you can do about the problem depends on what has gone wrong.

- You should check your universal credit award notice to make sure all the elements you are entitled to are included. There is more about the different elements in Chapter 5. If you think the award is wrong, you can ask the Department for Work and Pensions (DWP) to reconsider the decision. If you are still unhappy, you can usually appeal to an independent tribunal.

- If there is a delay in getting paid, or you are having difficulty waiting for your first payment, you may be able to get a 'short-term advance'. You should ask for this as soon as possible, ideally at your first appointment with your 'work coach'. There is more information about these payments in Chapter 4.

- If you are late making your claim, you may miss out on benefit. You may be able to get your award backdated. There is more about backdating in Chapter 4.

- If your circumstances have changed, you must report anything that might affect your universal credit, and any other changes you are told to report, as soon as possible. There is more information about changes in circumstances in Chapter 4.

- If you are told that you have been overpaid universal credit, you may have to repay it. First, you should check whether the overpayment is correct.

- If you have difficulty managing your money, you can ask for 'alternative payment arrangements'. These can include having your housing costs paid direct to your landlord, having smaller payments paid more frequently or having the payment split between you and your partner. There is more about alternative payment arrangements in Chapter 4. You can also ask your work coach if you can be referred for budgeting support.

- If your benefit is reduced because of a 'sanction', you can ask the DWP to reconsider the decision. If you are still unhappy, you can appeal. There is more information about sanctions in Chapter 7.

- If you are fined, you can ask the DWP to reconsider the decision. If you are still unhappy, you can appeal. There is more information about fines in Chapter 7.

2. What happens if you are overpaid?

If more universal credit is paid to you than you are entitled to, you have been overpaid.

There are many reasons why universal credit might be overpaid, including the following.

- You give the wrong information when you claim.

- You are late reporting a change of circumstances.

- Your employer gives the wrong details about your earnings when reporting these to HM Revenue and Customs (HMRC).

- The Department for Work and Pensions (DWP) makes a mistake when it works out your award or when it records the information you give.

- The DWP does not act on the information you give.

- The DWP does not pass on information from one department to another.

If your universal credit is overpaid, the DWP should do the following.

- **Change the decision.** If the overpayment is because of a change in your entitlement to universal credit, the DWP must usually 'revise' or 'supersede' the decision awarding you benefit. These are the legal ways in which the DWP can change a decision on your entitlement. In some circumstances, the DWP does not have to change the decision before recovering an overpayment – eg, if you are paid twice by mistake or if someone else receives a payment intended for you.

- Calculate the overpayment. Normally this is the difference between what you were paid and how much you should have been entitled to.

- Decide whether to recover the overpayment. The DWP can recover any overpayment, even when it is not your fault. However, the decision whether or not to do so is at its discretion.

- Decide who to recover the overpayment from. The general rule is that an overpayment can be recovered from the person to whom it was paid. If you claim jointly as a couple, it can be recovered from one or both of you, even if you are not the one who received the payment.

- Decide how to recover the overpayment. There are various methods the DWP can use to recover an overpayment.

EXAMPLES

Why overpayments happen

Parveen is working part time. Her employer has mixed up the details of her earnings with those of someone else and has told HMRC that she earns less than she does. When the mistake comes to light, the DWP revises her award. She has an overpayment of universal credit.

Wayne claims universal credit when he stops work because of cancer treatment. His partner moves in to look after him. He does not realise that he needs to inform the DWP. When he does tell the DWP some months later, he finds he has an overpayment of universal credit as Wayne and his partner should have claimed as a couple.

Anna has an award of universal credit of £300 a month. One month, there is a mix-up in the system and two sums of £300 are paid into her bank account on the same day by mistake. Anna queries it and is told that this is an overpayment.

What CPAG says

What can you do if you have been overpaid?

- Check your award carefully. If you disagree that you have been overpaid or with the amount you have been overpaid, ask for this to be reconsidered and then appeal if the DWP does not revise it. You can do this at the same time as disputing recovery, but you must make it clear that you are asking for a reconsideration of the amount of the overpayment and not whether it can be recovered.

- If paying back the overpayment will cause you hardship or affect your family's health or welfare, ask for some or all of it to be written off. If it was the DWP's fault not yours, explain this too.

- If the DWP does not do as you ask, you can consider using its internal complaints procedure.

- If you are still unhappy, you can take your case to the Independent Case Examiner. It deals with complaints about the DWP, and can make recommendations about how they should be settled.

- Contact your MP and ask for her/his help – eg, by taking the complaint to the Parliamentary and Health Service Ombudsman.

- In exceptional cases, you might be able to make a legal challenge, called a 'judicial review'. Get advice about this.

Do you have to repay an overpayment?

The DWP can ask you to pay back any overpayment, even if it was caused by a mistake by the DWP. This means that you cannot appeal against a decision to recover an overpayment. If, however, you believe that you were not overpaid, or that the amount is wrong, you can appeal after requesting a 'mandatory reconsideration'.

The DWP has a code of practice on overpayments. Under this, it asks for all overpayments to be paid back. In exceptional circumstances, the DWP may decide not to recover some or all of an overpayment – eg, if this could cause you or your family hardship and affect your health or welfare. The code of practice does not say that an overpayment will be written off just because it was the DWP's mistake. You could still ask for this, but you should also explain the effect on your family if you would have to repay it.

Although you cannot appeal against a decision to recover an overpayment, if you think you should not have to pay it back, you can 'dispute' it.

EXAMPLE

Disputing an overpayment

Dot has separated from her partner Ian, who has moved out of the family home. The relationship has been off and on for a while and Dot hoped he would be back. She is feeling depressed and anxious. Six months later, Dot tells the DWP that Ian has gone. The DWP revises her universal credit award from the date that Ian moved out and works out how much she has been overpaid. She is told that amounts to repay this overpayment will be deducted each month from her award. Dot thinks this will leave her with insufficient money. She does three things.

• She checks her award and discovers the DWP has taken the date of separation as the date Ian moved out. If they were not sure if the separation was permanent at that date, Dot could argue that it was only a temporary separation and that they remained entitled to universal credit as a couple until they had decided to separate permanently.

• She asks the DWP to write off the overpayment because the repayments are causing her hardship and her mental ill health makes it very hard for her to deal with problems, including reporting changes that affect her benefit at the right time.

• She gets advice from an advice centre. An adviser helps her with the dispute and appeal.

How do you repay an overpayment?

The DWP can recover overpayments of universal credit by:

- making deductions from an ongoing award of benefit you have
- reducing an amount of arrears of benefit that is owed to you
- making deductions from your earnings
- taking court action against you

The usual way of repaying an overpayment is from your ongoing award of benefit. This might be universal credit or it might be another benefit. Deductions can be made from most benefits, but not from child benefit or guardian's allowance. The maximum amount that can be deducted from your universal credit for an overpayment is normally 15 per cent of your 'standard allowance'. However, it can be more than this if you have earnings, if fraud is involved or if 'hardship payments' are being recovered.

If you are employed, the DWP can recover an overpayment of universal credit from your earnings. The DWP sends a notice to you and your employer to say how much will be deducted. No deduction is made if your net earnings are less than £100 a week or £430 a month (in 2017/18), unless the overpayment is connected to an offence for which you have been found guilty. You employer can also deduct up to a £1 administration charge from your earnings each time it makes a deduction for an overpayment.

The DWP can recover an overpayment of universal credit through the courts. It might do so if it cannot recover in another way – eg, if you are not receiving any benefits and not working. Court costs can be added to the overpayment and treated as part of it. There are time limits in which the DWP must start court action. There is no time limit for recovering overpayments in other ways.

EXAMPLE

Repaying an overpayment

Mona has been getting universal credit as someone with 'limited capability for work', but starts a part-time job. Her award is adjusted. A year later, the DWP decides it has miscalculated her entitlement since she started working. Her award is reassessed and the amount she has been overpaid is worked out. The DWP decides to recover the overpayment and to do so from both her ongoing universal credit award and her earnings, as her current award is low and the rate of recovery from her earnings will not cause her hardship. Her employer makes the deductions the DWP has requested from Mona's wages.

3. Do you disagree with a decision?

If you disagree with a decision about your universal credit, you can formally challenge it.

First, you should ask the Department for Work and Pensions (DWP) to look at its decision again. This is called asking for a 'mandatory reconsideration' (the legal term is 'revision'). The DWP can revise a decision if you ask for this within a month of the date the decision was sent to you. If it has been longer than a month, a decision can still be revised if there are special reasons to extend the time limit, or if it can be revised or 'superseded' (another legal way to change a decision) on particular grounds.

Once the DWP makes a decision, it should send you a 'mandatory reconsideration notice' explaining your right to appeal if you are still not happy. You can appeal against most decisions, but not about whether to recover an overpayment or what your 'work-related requirements' are. Once you have this notice, you can then appeal to an independent appeal tribunal.

There are strict time limits for appealing. You should appeal within one month of being sent the mandatory reconsideration notice, although the time limits can be extended for special reasons. You should appeal by completing form SSCS1 which is available from www.gov.uk.

EXAMPLE

Disagreeing with a decision

Ilona gets universal credit for herself and her child. She has mental health problems and has been getting an additional element in her award for being ill. At her next medical examination, she is assessed as being fit for work. She receives a decision saying that her universal credit award will no longer include the additional element. Ilona believes she is too ill to work and wants to challenge this. She is not sure how to do so and contacts the DWP to say she wants to appeal. Because the rules say she must first ask for a revision, the DWP treats this as a request to consider revising the decision. After reconsidering the decision, the DWP decides not to revise it. Ilona can now appeal. She makes her written appeal immediately so she does not miss the deadline, and goes to her local advice centre for help to make her case.

---

4. How do you complain?

If you disagree with a decision on your universal credit award or payment, first check whether you can ask for this to be changed by using the 'revision' and appeal process.

If you are unhappy with the way your universal credit claim has been handled, you can make a complaint. For instance, you may want to complain about:

- a delay in dealing with your claim
- poor administration in the benefit office
- poor advice from the Department for Work and Pensions (DWP)
- poor administration or advice from staff helping you look for or prepare for work

- a poorly conducted medical examination
- the way the system affects you

How do you complain about the Department for Work and Pensions?

If you are unhappy with the way your claim has been handled, you should first take this up with the office dealing with it. Contact details should be on any letters you have about your claim. If this does not resolve the issue, the DWP has a complaints procedure. This can be found at www.gov.uk.

Once you have gone through all the steps in the complaints procedure, if you are still unhappy with the response, you can take your case to the Independent Case Examiner. This deals with complaints about the DWP and its contracted providers. It can settle complaints by agreement between you and the DWP or carry out an investigation and make recommendations about how a complaint should be settled.

If you are still not happy, you can contact your MP and ask her/him to refer your complaint to the Parliamentary and Health Service Ombudsman.

How do you complain about a 'contracted' provider?

If you are unhappy with the service, advice or administration from a provider contracted by the DWP to carry out employment support services, you should first contact the provider. If you use its complaints procedure and you are not satisfied with the response, you can then complain to the Independent Case Examiner, and if you are still not happy, contact your MP and ask her/him to refer your complaint to the Ombudsman.

How do you complain about a medical examination?

DWP medical examinations are conducted by contracted providers such as Maximus Health, Atos or Capita. To complain about the conduct of a medical examination or about the healthcare professional who carried it out, contact the provider and use its complaints procedure. If you are not satisfied with the response, you can complain to the Independent Case Examiner. If you are still unhappy, ask your MP to refer your complaint to the Ombudsman.

How do you use your MP?

If you do not have a particular universal credit issue to resolve, but you are unhappy with the way the system affects you, you may wish to take this up with your local MP.

You can also take up a specific problem with your MP. Usually it is best to do this if you have already tried to resolve the problem directly with the DWP, but are still dissatisfied. In particular, it can be useful to ask your MP for help if there has been a delay in your claim being dealt with.

You can email or write to your MP, or go to a local 'surgery' – ie, the regular sessions that MPs usually have to meet their constituents.

Further information

The DWP has produced a code of practice called *What Happens If You Are Overpaid Universal Credit, Jobseeker's Allowance or Employment and Support Allowance?* (COP1), which is available at www.gov.uk.
For information and tactical tips on appeals, see CPAG's guide *Winning Your Benefit Appeal: what you need to know*.
To find out who your MP is and how to contact her/him, see www.parliament.uk. You can also find contact details in your local library or town hall, or you can write to your local MP at the House of Commons, London SW1A 0AA.

Other useful contacts:

Customer Relations Team
Health Assessment Advisory Service (Maximus)
Room 4E04
Quarry House,
Quarry Hill
Leeds LS2 7UA
Tel: 0800 288 8777
email: customer-relations@chdauk.co.uk
www.chdauk.co.uk

Parliamentary and Health Service Ombudsman
Millbank Tower
Millbank
London SW1P 4QP
Tel: 0345 015 4033
www.ombudsman.org.uk

Independent Case Examiner
PO Box 209
Bootle L20 7WA
Tel: 0345 606 0777
email: ice@dwp.gsi.gov.uk
www.gov.uk/government/organisations/independent-case-examiner

Chapter 9
Universal credit and specific groups of people

This chapter covers:

1. Lone parents

2. Families with three or more children

3. People in work

4. Carers

5. Disabled people

6. Young people

7. Older people

8. People from abroad

What you need to know

- You can only claim universal credit if you live in a 'full service' area, or in a 'live service' area and you meet the 'gateway' conditions. Currently, these gateway conditions mean you cannot make a claim if you are disabled, 60 and six months or over, not a UK citizen, or if you are caring for a severely disabled person. In most areas, you also cannot claim if you have a partner or a child.

- Once universal credit is fully introduced, anyone can claim provided they meet the basic rules of entitlement and the financial conditions. Your personal or family circumstances determine how much you get and what requirements you must meet.

- The 'work-related requirements' that lone parents must meet to get universal credit vary, depending on the age of their youngest child.

- Up until 31 October 2018, families with three or more children will not be able to make a new claim for universal credit.

- You can claim universal credit both in and out of work. If your earnings are low you may still have 'work-related requirements'.

- Full-time carers have no work-related requirements and may be entitled to an additional amount of universal credit.

- Disabled people must usually have a medical assessment of their ability to work or to prepare for work. Their work-related requirements depend on the extent of their disability. Some may qualify for an additional amount.

- Special rules allow some 16/17-year-olds and some young people in education to claim universal credit.

- People over the qualifying age for pension credit cannot generally get universal credit.

- Certain people from abroad are excluded from universal credit.

1. Lone parents

Can lone parents claim universal credit?

Lone parents can claim universal credit in 'full service' areas, and in 'live service' areas where the 'gateway' conditions currently allow claims from people with children. Chapter 2 has more information on this.

You are a lone parent if you are responsible for a child who normally lives with you and you do not have a partner living with you.

If you are a lone parent, you make a single claim for universal credit, but you must make a joint claim as a couple if you have a partner living with you. It is important to be clear about whether you are a lone parent and be aware that if a partner moves in with you, even if s/he is not the parent of your child, you become a couple and have a joint universal credit award.

Are there any special rules?

If you are a lone parent, the maximum amount of universal credit payable to you is based on an allowance for yourself and your children, plus an amount for housing costs and, if you are in work, an amount for your childcare costs. There are additional amounts if you care for a disabled child or adult, or if you or your child are disabled. There is no additional amount specifically for lone parents. However, as a parent, you get a 'work allowance', which is the amount you can earn before your universal credit is reduced. There is more information on how universal credit is calculated in Chapter 5.

If you share the care of your children with a former partner, it is not possible to split payments for children. You can agree who should claim for your child or, if you cannot agree, the Department for Work and Pensions (DWP) decides which one of you has the main responsibility. This does not automatically go to who claimed first, or who gets child benefit, but takes into account a range of factors. If it is decided that you do not have main responsibility for a child, you are not treated as a lone parent. This means you are not entitled to additional amounts for a child, you are subject to the 'work-related requirements' that apply to your other circumstances, and the amount you can get to help with your rent may be reduced if you have a spare bedroom for a child to stay with you.

Note: there are special rules if you have three or more children. These are explained on page 132.

If you do not comply with your work-related requirements, the amount of your universal credit may be reduced ('sanctioned'). There is more information about sanctions in Chapter 7.

There are exceptions to work-related requirements if you have experienced domestic violence within the previous six months.

Your work-related requirements

Your work-related requirements depend on the age of your youngest child.

Box A
Lone parents and looking for work

- If you have a child under the age of one, you have no work-related requirements, so you can look after your new baby and get universal credit without having to worry about work during the first year.

- If you have a child aged one, you must attend 'work-focused interviews', usually every six months, to discuss your employability.

- If you have a child aged two, you must attend 'work-focused interviews' and you are also required to prepare for work. This involves undertaking activity that makes it more likely that you will return to work in the future.

- Once your youngest child turns three, you have all the work-related requirements, which means you must look for work and be available to take up a job. You are allowed to place some restrictions on the type of work and the hours you are prepared to do.

- As long as you have a child aged under 13, you can limit your expected hours of work to fit in with your child's normal school or nursery hours including travel, so you only need to be available for work while s/he is at school or nursery.

- Most people are required to attend an interview or take up a job immediately. As a lone parent, you may be allowed up to one month's notice to take up work or 48 hours' notice to attend an interview, taking into account how long you need to arrange childcare.

> **EXAMPLE**
>
> **Lone parent**
>
> Martha is a lone parent with one child aged six. She gets universal credit and must search for work and be available for work. Her 'claimant commitment' allows her to restrict her availability to school hours during term time only. She is asked to attend a skills assessment course for two weeks while her child is at school. If she refuses to go, her universal credit is likely to be sanctioned. She is offered a temporary job of four hours a day during school hours, three days a week. If she does not accept the job, she may receive a sanction. The job continues to be available during the school holidays. Martha can get help with 85 per cent of her childcare costs in her universal credit, so she can continue working. If suitable childcare is not available, she should not receive a sanction for giving up the job.

Childcare costs

Universal credit may include an amount to help with your childcare costs if you are paying a registered childcare provider, such as a childminder, nursery or after-school club.

There is no minimum number of hours you must work to qualify for help with childcare; any work can qualify, provided the amount of childcare is not considered excessive in relation to how many hours you work.

The full costs of your childcare are not covered – only 85 per cent of the costs are covered, up to a maximum payment of £646 a month for one child or £1,108 for two or more children.

You can claim childcare costs before starting work if you have been offered a job that is due to start in the following 'assessment period', to allow a settling-in period for your child. Childcare costs can include deposits or up-front fees, but remember that universal credit is paid in arrears. You cannot claim for an amount that is paid or reimbursed by your employer or someone else, or covered by other support. You can continue to claim childcare costs for one assessment period after stopping work, to allow you to find another job without losing the childcare place.

You must report your actual childcare costs on a monthly basis. If you do not report them by the end of the following month, they cannot be met. It is your responsibility to report your childcare costs, not the childcare provider's, although your provider may be required to confirm the costs. There is no system of automatic notification as with earnings.

Other benefits for lone parents

- **Child benefit** remains outside the universal credit system, and is administered by HM Revenue and Customs. You should claim child benefit for your children, as well as universal credit. You do not have to claim child benefit to prove that you are responsible for a child for universal credit.

- Lone parents who have been bereaved can claim **bereavement support payment** (or widowed parent's allowance if their spouse or civil partner died before 6 April 2017). Bereavement support payment is not taken into account as income when your universal credit is assessed (but widowed parent's allowance counts as unearned income and is deducted in full from your universal credit).

- You can get a **Sure Start maternity grant** if you get universal credit. This is £500 to help with the costs of a new baby, but it is usually only payable for your first child. It does not matter about other income or whether you are in work, provided you are entitled to universal credit.

- If you are pregnant or have a child under four and you get universal credit and have a family take-home pay of £408 or less a month, you should qualify for **Healthy Start vouchers** for milk, fruit and vegetables, and free vitamins. Telephone the Healthy Start helpline for more information.

2. Families with three or more children

Can families with three or more children claim universal credit?

In April 2017, the government introduced a 'two-child limit' to 'means-tested benefits'. If your family has three or more children, you cannot make a new claim for universal credit between 6 April 2017 and 31 October 2018 unless you have been in receipt of universal credit within the previous six-month period and are making a reclaim. Instead, you are directed to claim tax credits and the other old means-tested benefits.

If you are already getting universal credit on 6 April 2017, or you make a reclaim within six months of a previous claim, you get an amount in your universal credit for any children that were part of your household before 6 April 2017. However, a child element is not included in your award for any 'third or subsequent child' who becomes part of your household on or after 6 April 2017, unless an exception in Box B applies.

From 1 November 2018, it is expected that new claims for universal credit will be accepted from any family but, unless an exception in Box B applies, a child element will not be included for any third or subsequent children in the household, regardless of when they were born or joined the household. However, it is intended that households who have been in receipt of support for children in tax credits in the last month, or universal credit in the last six months, will be protected so that their existing level of entitlement is maintained as long as they remain responsible for the same children. The rules had not been finalised at the time this book was written.

Are there any special rules?

Even if you cannot have a child element included in your universal credit award for a third or subsequent child, you can still have the disabled child element included for that child, if applicable, and you can also receive help with the childcare costs for that child, subject to the normal rules described in Chapter 5.

It is also possible to have a child element included for a third or subsequent child if an exception applies.

Box B
Exceptions to the 'two-child limit'

- **Multiple birth** – if the child is born in a multiple birth, and there are already two or more children in the household, an exception applies to all but one of the children. If any of the children in the multiple birth are the first or second child in the household, a child element is automatically awarded for her/him, and an exception applies to any others born as part of the same birth.

- **Adopted children** – if you adopt a child who would otherwise be in local authority care, and that child is a third or subsequent child in your household, an exception applies to that child.

- **Friend and family carers** – if you look after a child informally or under a formal caring arrangement and the child would otherwise be looked after by a local authority, and that child is a third or subsequent child in your household, an exception applies to that child.

- **Under 16s who have a child** – if a child under 16 in your household becomes the parent of a child, and you are responsible for the new child who is a third or subsequent child in your household, an exception applies to that child.

- **Non-consensual conception** – if you have a third or subsequent child who is likely to have been conceived as a result of rape or in a 'controlling or coercive relationship', an exception applies to that child. You must not be living at the same address as the alleged perpetrator for the exception to apply.

In the case of adopted children and 'friend and family carers', the date when parental responsibility passes to you is used as the date the child joined the household for the purposes of deciding whether s/he is a third or subsequent child. However, if you give birth to a child within 10 months of having taken responsibility for a child who would meet the non-parental care exception criteria, you can choose in which order to place the two children so as to get the maximum universal credit.

EXAMPLES

The 'two-child limit'

Penny is in receipt of universal credit and has two children. She gives birth to twins on 30 September 2017. A child element is not paid for the first twin but an exception applies to the other twin. Penny's universal credit award includes three child elements in total.

Mark and Mary get universal credit. They have one child who is aged six and they took responsibility for Mary's niece, Bethan, in May 2017. In September 2017, Mary gives birth to another child, Harry. Because Harry is born within 10 months of Bethan joining the household, Mark and Mary can choose in which order they are counted. Harry is selected as the second child and Bethan as the third child because an exception applies to her. Mark and Mary have three child elements included in their universal credit award.

3. People in work

Can people in work claim universal credit?

You can claim universal credit both in and out of work, although your earnings affect how much you can get. There is more information about how your earnings are assessed in Chapter 5. There is no need to make a new claim as you move in and out of work but you must tell the Department for Work and Pensions (DWP) if you start or finish work.

Are there any special rules?

If you are employed, you do not have to report your earnings as your employer is required to report your earnings every time you are paid. If you are self-employed, there are special rules about reporting your income every month. Also, if you have a low income and you have been self-employed for over a year, you may be assumed to have higher earnings than you do. There is more information about how your earnings are treated in Chapter 5.

If you have children or have been assessed as having 'limited capability for work or work-related activity', some of your earnings are ignored when calculating your universal credit. This is called the 'work allowance'. There is more information about how your universal credit is calculated in Chapter 5.

Your work-related requirements

Even though you are working, you may still be required to look for further work, or increase your hours, if your earnings are below the 'earnings threshold'. There is more information about your 'claimant commitment' and 'work-related requirements' in Chapter 6.

If you do not comply with your work-related requirements, the amount of your universal credit may be reduced ('sanctioned'). There is more information about sanctions in Chapter 7.

EXAMPLE

Single person working

Joshua has been claiming universal credit as a jobseeker. He gets a job working three days a week at the minimum wage. He tells the DWP that he has started work and his employer reports his earnings each month, so his universal credit is reassessed to take his earnings into account. His 'work coach' reviews his claimant commitment as Joshua is in work. Although he is in work for 24 hours a week, Joshua is expected to spend a further 11 hours looking for additional or better paid work.

4. Carers

Can carers claim universal credit?

Carers looking after a severely disabled person can claim universal credit in 'full service' areas. Chapter 2 has more information on this.

Under universal credit, there are special rules if you are caring for a severely disabled person and you are not paid to provide care. To be recognised as severely disabled, the person you look after must get the middle or highest rate of the disability living allowance care component, either rate of the daily living component of personal independence payment or either rate of attendance allowance. You can be recognised as a carer for universal credit even if you do not get carer's allowance.

Are there any special rules?

There is an additional amount in universal credit (a 'carer element') for people who have 'regular and substantial' caring responsibilities for a severely disabled person. This means that you provide care for at least 35 hours a week.

You can get the carer element whether or not you have made a claim for carer's allowance.

Before applying, bear in mind that getting a carer element could mean that the person you care for gets less benefit. This is because the severe disability addition sometimes paid in other benefits like pension credit and employment and support allowance will stop.

If more than one person is caring for the same disabled person, the carer element can only be paid to one of you. If you are in a couple and you are both carers, you can get two carer elements, but you must be looking after different people. If you both look after the same person, you should decide who is the main carer or the Department for Work and Pensions (DWP) will decide for you, and the other partner will usually have to look for work.

If you are also disabled, you cannot get the carer element at the same time as the additional amount paid because of your disability (a 'limited capability for work' or 'limited capability for work-related activity' element). If you are a disabled carer, you should make this clear in your claim and the DWP must award the element of the highest value. If you are in a couple, you can get a carer element for yourself and a limited capability for work or limited capability for work-related activity element for your disabled partner.

Carers who are in work have their overall universal credit award reduced, in the same way as other claimants. There is no extra 'work allowance' for carers. However, you do not lose the carer element just because you are working (even if you earn more than the limit for carer's allowance – £116 in 2017/18), provided you are still caring for at least 35 hours a week.

Carers who spend at least 35 hours a week caring for a severely disabled person do not have any 'work-related requirements', so you can get universal credit without being expected to look for work. You may also have no work-related requirements in the following circumstances.

• You care for more than one severely disabled person and your total caring responsibilities amount to at least 35 hours a week.

• You care for a severely disabled person for at least 35 hours a week, but you are not the main carer, perhaps because someone else gets a carer element for looking after her/him.

In these situations, the DWP must be satisfied that it is unreasonable to expect you to look for work, even within agreed limits. However, you do not get the carer element.

If you spend less than 35 hours a week caring, or you care for a disabled person who does not get the middle or highest rate of the disability living allowance care component, either rate of the daily living component of personal independence payment or either rate of attendance allowance, you are expected to look for work, within limits if agreed in your 'claimant commitment'. You can restrict the hours you are available for, and looking for, work so that this is compatible with your caring responsibilities, provided this is agreed and you still have a reasonable chance of finding work. This may also apply if the disabled person is waiting to hear about a new claim for personal independence payment or attendance allowance. However, there is no rule that automatically treats you as a carer while her/his claim is being decided, so any flexibility in your work-related requirements must be agreed in your claimant commitment.

EXAMPLES

Carers

Duncan is a carer for his brother, who gets the daily living component of personal independence payment. Duncan gets universal credit and has no work-related requirements. His brother's personal independence payment stops following a review. Duncan no longer meets the conditions as a carer for a severely disabled person, so he has all the work-related requirements. He is able to agree some restrictions in his claimant commitment on his hours of availability for work and the notice required to attend an interview or take up a job. His 'work coach' must be satisfied that his brother still has a disability. Duncan must still show that he is taking all reasonable action to find work within the agreed restrictions, otherwise his universal credit may be 'sanctioned'.

Sue and Richard care for their daughter who gets the middle rate care component of disability living allowance. Sue works and Richard has limited capability for work-related activity. Although both Sue and Richard are carers they nominate Sue as the main carer. Their universal credit award includes the carer element for Sue and the limited capability for work-related activity element for Richard. If they had nominated Richard as the main carer, the award would only have included the limited capability for work-related activity element as the two elements cannot be awarded in respect of the same person.

Box C
Foster carers

- Foster carers who are legally approved to look after a child or young person by arrangement with a local authority or voluntary organisation are treated differently from carers looking after a disabled person.

- In Scotland, approved kinship carers are treated in the same way as foster carers.

- There are special rules for foster carers in universal credit.

- Lone foster carers are only required to attend 'work-focused interviews'. They do not have any other work-related requirements until their youngest foster child reaches 16, when they are required to look for, and be available for, work.

- In exceptional circumstances when a foster child who is 16 or 17 needs full-time care, the foster carer is only required to participate in work-focused interviews and has no other work-related requirements, until the child reaches 18 or the placement ends.

- Fostering couples must say which one of the couple is the lead carer. The lead carer is only required to attend work-focused interviews and has no other work-related requirements. The other member of the couple has all the work-related requirements that apply in her/his circumstances, unless there are exceptional circumstances and the foster child needs full-time care by two adults.

- Fostering is not treated as being self-employed or in work.

- Fostering payments are not taken into account as earnings or income. There is no additional amount in universal credit for being a foster carer.

Other benefits for carers

Carers can claim **carer's allowance**. You must spend at least 35 hours a week looking after a severely disabled person who gets the middle or higher rate of disability living allowance care component, either rate of the daily living component of personal independence payment, or either rate of attendance allowance. You cannot get carer's allowance if you are a full-time student or if you earn over £116 a week (in 2017/18).

Carer's allowance counts as income in full for universal credit. However, it is not enough to live on, so you may get a top-up of universal credit as well. If you have claimed carer's allowance and meet the conditions, but have been told that it cannot be paid because you get another benefit (such as contributory employment and support allowance), you can still be treated as a carer for universal credit. If you are earning over £116 a week, but you meet the other conditions for carer's allowance, you can still be treated as a carer for universal credit, even if you have not actually claimed carer's allowance.

5. Disabled people

Can disabled people claim universal credit?

People with disabilities can claim universal credit in 'full service' areas. There is more information on this in Chapter 2.

You may be entitled to an extra amount in your universal credit if you are disabled. There are different rules for adults and children.

Are there any special rules?

There are special rules for some people with disabilities. These affect how much universal credit you get, what kind of 'work-related requirements' you have and, if you work, how much of your earnings you can keep before your universal credit is affected.

Universal credit can include additional amounts for disabled adults and children paid at either of two rates, depending on the severity of the disability. However, the criteria are different for adults and children.

The additional amount you get for a disabled child depends on the amount of disability living allowance or personal independence payment s/he gets. This is explained in Chapter 5.

The additional amount you get as a disabled adult (a 'limited capability for work' or 'limited capability for work-related activity element') depends on a medical assessment of your capability for work. This 'limited capability for work test' is explained in Chapter 5.

Note: you cannot get the limited capability for work element if your period of limited capability for work started on or after 3 April 2017.

The additional amount for adults is not related to disability living allowance or personal independence payment, and it does not make any difference whether you live alone or have a carer. There is only one additional amount for a couple, even if both of you are sick or disabled.

If you are disabled and you also care for someone who is disabled, you cannot get an additional amount for your disability as well as a 'carer element' for yourself in your universal credit. However, if you are in a couple and you are disabled and your partner is a carer, you can get a limited capability for work or a limited capability for work-related activity element for yourself and a carer element for your partner.

Disabled people can earn more than some other claimants before their universal credit is reduced. This is called a 'work allowance'. You qualify for this disregard if you or your partner have been assessed as having limited capability for work or work-related activity.

If you are a disabled person getting universal credit and you start work, you do not automatically stop having limited capability for work or work-related activity, so you do not necessarily lose the additional amount and work allowance, but your capability for work may be reassessed.

If you become disabled while you are in work and your weekly earnings are at least 16 times the national minimum wage, you can only be newly assessed as having limited capability for work or work-related activity in order to get the additional amount in your universal credit or a higher work allowance if you get disability living allowance or personal independence payment.

EXAMPLE

Disabled person

Sarah is a single person who has previously been in good health, working 20 hours a week on the minimum wage. She gets universal credit, but is expected to look for better paid work or more hours. She is diagnosed with a long-term health condition and believes that this is affecting her ability to work. She does not want to give up her job, but feels that she should be entitled to additional support through universal credit as a disabled worker. She asks to be assessed for limited capability for work, which would give her more to live on, allow more of her earnings to be ignored, and she would not have to look for more work. Her request is refused because she is already working more than 16 hours a week. She must therefore first apply for personal independence payment. If this is awarded, she can then be assessed for limited capability for work for universal credit.

Other benefits for disabled people

- You can claim **contributory employment and support allowance** if you have worked and paid enough national insurance contributions, although payment may be limited to one year. You may be entitled to contributory employment and support allowance at the same time as universal credit, but contributory employment and support allowance counts in full as income for universal credit, so it reduces your entitlement. In some situations, you can get contributory employment and support allowance if you cannot get universal credit – eg, if your savings are too high. If you are entitled to contributory employment and support allowance and universal credit, or you move from one to another, the rules on work-related requirements, 'sanctions' and 'hardship payments' apply to both benefits.

- You can claim **personal independence payment** if you have a disability which affects your mobility or ability to carry out daily living activities. Personal independence payment is replacing disability living allowance for people aged 16 to 64, but if your child is disabled you should still claim **disability living allowance**. You can continue to receive disability living allowance or personal independence payment in addition to your universal credit, as these remain outside the universal credit system and do not count as income.

6. Young people

Can young people claim universal credit?

One of the basic rules for universal credit is that you must be aged at least 18 to claim. However, if you live in a 'full service' area, there are special rules that allow some young people aged 16 and 17 to claim universal credit. See Chapter 2 for more information on this.

If you are aged under 16, you cannot claim universal credit in any circumstances. A responsible adult with whom you live should claim for you, or the local authority must have responsibility for you. If you are aged 18 to 21 and make a new claim in a 'full service' area, you may not be able to get the housing costs element of universal credit for your rent. There is more about this in Chapter 5.

Are there any special rules?

If you are aged 16 or 17, you can claim universal credit for yourself, any housing costs you are liable for and any children you are responsible for if:

- you have a child or are about to have a baby
- you are 'without parental support'
- you are disabled or ill
- you are a carer

Chapter 3 explains more about when you can claim in these situations.

If you are a care leaver aged 16 or 17, you cannot usually get universal credit and the local authority still has a duty to support you. You can only get universal credit as a care leaver if you are disabled or responsible for a child.

If you are still in education, you may be classed as a student and so cannot get universal credit. More information about studying is in Chapter 3.

EXAMPLE

Young person estranged from parents

Zoe is aged 17 and has recently left school and started work. She has an argument with her parents and leaves home. She finds a room in private rented accommodation, and claims universal credit because she lives in a 'full service' area. She is below the normal qualifying age of 18, and must make a statement explaining that she is estranged from her parents. The Department for Work and Pensions looks at her statement and its own guidance, which says there is no requirement to corroborate such evidence or contact parents. Zoe should be believed, unless her statement is self-contradictory or improbable.

Young people under the age of 25 get less universal credit than people aged 25 and over. In addition, from April 2017, young people aged 18 to 21 in 'full service' areas are not entitled to the 'housing costs element' of universal credit, although there are exceptions – eg, for vulnerable young people who cannot live with their parents, or for a limited time to allow people to look for work after a job has ended. In addition, 18–21-year-olds in 'full service' areas have to take part in a Youth Obligation programme, with more 'work-related requirements', including applying for an apprenticeship, traineeship, work experience or work placement.

Other benefits for young people

There are not many other benefits that young people aged 16 or 17 can claim for themselves. If you are disabled, you may be able to claim personal independence payment. If you are a carer, you may be able to claim carer's allowance. You can only claim 'contributory benefits', such as employment and support allowance or jobseeker's allowance, if you have worked and paid enough national insurance contributions, usually for two to three years before you claim.

7. Older people

Can older people claim universal credit?

Older people aged 60 years and six months or over can only claim universal credit if they live in a 'full service' area. Chapter 2 has more information on this.

Even if you or your partner are younger than this when you claim, one of the basic rules of entitlement to universal credit is that you have not reached the qualifying age for pension credit. This is 64 for both men and women in July 2017, gradually rising to 66 by October 2020.

So, if you are single, you cannot stay on universal credit when you reach pension credit age. If you are in a couple, when one of you reaches pension credit age, you should be able to choose between staying on universal credit or claiming pension credit. You cannot get both. You will normally be better off on pension credit.

Are there any special rules?

There is no additional amount for older people in universal credit. A couple with one partner over the qualifying age for pension credit gets less money on universal credit than on pension credit.

If a couple is claiming universal credit, only the working-age partner has 'work-related requirements'. However, if the working-age partner fails to meet her/his requirements, the couple may still be 'sanctioned', which means losing half of their universal credit 'standard allowance' for a period of time.

Other benefits for older people

- Universal credit does not replace **pension credit**. You cannot get pension credit and universal credit at the same time. You may be entitled to one, but not the other. In the future, it is intended that pension credit will change to include additional amounts for rent and for children, replacing housing benefit and child tax credit. It is also expected that the qualifying rules for pension credit will change so that both members of a couple must have reached the qualifying age.

- Universal credit does not replace **retirement pension**. If you get retirement pension and your partner is under the qualifying age for pension credit, you can get universal credit, but retirement pension is counted in full as income.

- **Attendance allowance** and the **winter fuel payment** remain outside the universal credit system and are not counted as income when working out how much universal credit you get.

EXAMPLE

Older people

Jacob and Sandra are 64 and 58 and claim universal credit as a couple. Both are healthy and their claimant commitments include all work-related requirements. They own their own home so have no housing costs. When Jacob is 65 they can choose whether to stay on universal credit or claim pension credit instead.

They decide to claim pension credit. Their weekly benefit is £243.25 and neither of them have any work-related requirements.

If they had stayed on universal credit their monthly benefit would have been £498.89 – equivalent to £115.13 a week. Although Jacob's claimant commitment has no work-related requirements, Sandra's claimant commitment would still have included all work-related requirements and she would be a risk of a sanction if she failed to meet them.

8. People from abroad

Can people from abroad claim universal credit?

You can only claim universal credit as a person from abroad in a 'full service' area. See Chapter 2 for more information on this.

You can only get universal credit if you meet the immigration and residence conditions.

The immigration conditions apply to people from countries outside the European Economic Area. You meet these conditions for universal credit if, for example, you are allowed to stay in the UK indefinitely without restrictions, or the UK government has recognised you as a refugee (but not while you are an asylum seeker) or granted you humanitarian protection or exceptional leave to enter or remain in the UK. You do not meet them if your entry clearance to the UK says you have 'no recourse to public funds'. This is usually stamped in your passport or on your biometric residence permit. Universal credit counts as 'public funds'.

If you are unsure about how claiming might affect your position, get specialist immigration advice.

Nationals of European Economic Area countries must have a 'right to reside' in the UK. Normally, this means you are working or self-employed in the UK. However, there are some other types of right to reside. For example, you may have a permanent right to reside, which usually means you have lived in the UK for over five years. If your only right to reside is as a jobseeker, you cannot get universal credit.

You must also be 'habitually resident' in the UK. This includes showing that you are settled in the UK and, usually, that you have been in the UK for at least one to three months. This also applies to British citizens returning to the UK from living abroad.

EXAMPLE

Person from abroad

Mika is a Polish national who came to the UK to work, and was working continuously for five years before losing her job. Her new partner, Brody, gets universal credit. Mika meets the residence conditions because, even though she is a jobseeker, she has been working continuously for five years and has a permanent right to reside. They claim universal credit as a couple.

Other benefits for people from abroad

There are special rules for certain groups of people from abroad for most other benefits.

Further information

There is more information about the rules for current benefits and tax credits in CPAG's *Welfare Benefits and Tax Credits Handbook.*
The Healthy Start helpline number is 0345 607 6823.

Appendix

Glossary of terms

Alternative payment arrangements
The discretion to pay universal credit twice a month, directly to a landlord or split between partners.

Appointee
Someone, usually a relative, who is authorised by the Department for Work and Pensions to claim benefit on another person's behalf if that person cannot claim for her/himself – eg, perhaps because of a learning disability.

Assessment period
The monthly period on which universal credit payment is based. You are paid up to seven days after the end of each assessment period.

'Bedroom tax'
A reduction in the amount of the housing costs element for tenants of local authorities and housing associations who have a spare bedroom(s).

Benefit cap
The maximum amount of social security benefits that someone can receive. This includes most benefits, but there are some exceptions and some groups to whom the cap does not apply.

Budgeting advance
An advance payment of universal credit in the form of a loan, usually for people who have been on benefits for at least six months.

Capital
This includes savings, investments, certain lump-sum payments and property which is not a person's main home.

Civil penalty
A fine that can be imposed if someone is overpaid a benefit because s/he failed to provide information or gave incorrect information, and is not being prosecuted for fraud or another benefit offence.

Claimant commitment
A document setting out what someone must do while claiming universal credit, and the possible penalties if its terms are not met.

Conditionality
What claimants are required to do in return for their benefit.

Contributory benefit
A benefit for which entitlement depends on having paid a certain amount of national insurance contributions.

Controlling or coercive relationship
A relationship where a partner uses controlling or coercive behaviour. Coercive behaviour includes assault, threats, humiliation or intimidation. Controlling behaviour isolates a person from sources of support and takes away her/his independence.

Couple
Two people living together who are married or civil partners, or living together as if they were a married couple or civil partners.

Discretionary housing payment
A payment that can be made by a local authority to top up universal credit when someone needs extra help with her/his housing costs.

Earnings threshold
The amount of a person's earnings (or joint earnings for couples) above which there is no expectation to look for more work, or meet any other work-related requirements.

Elements
Amounts for children, disabilities, caring responsibilities, housing and childcare which make up part of a person's maximum universal credit award.

European Economic Area
The 28 European Union member states, plus Iceland, Norway and Liechtenstein. For benefit purposes, Switzerland is also treated as part of the European Economic Area.

Friend and family carer
A person who has taken responsibility for a child of a friend or family member under a formal caring arrangement, or an informal caring arrangement where it is likely the child would otherwise be looked after by the local authority.

'Full service' area
An area where universal credit has been introduced with no 'gateway' conditions, and in which claimants have access to an electronic account in which they can view their payment details, report changes in their circumstances and provide evidence that they are meeting their 'claimant commitment'.

'Gateway' conditions
Criteria which permit only certain people to claim universal credit, in order to allow the Department for Work and Pensions to introduce universal credit gradually.

Habitually resident
Someone who has a settled intention to stay in the UK, and who has usually been living here for a period.

Hardship payments
Loans of universal credit made if someone's entitlement has been reduced by a sanction and s/he faces financial hardship.

Health and work conversation
A conversation with a work coach about a person's health issues and what support s/he needs.

Independent Case Examiner
A body handling complaints about the Department for Work and Pensions.

Judicial review
A way of challenging the decisions of government departments, local authorities and some tribunals against which there is no right of appeal.

Limited capability for work
A test of whether a person's ability to work is limited by a health condition.

Limited capability for work-related activity
A test of how severe a person's health problems are and whether her/his ability to prepare for work is limited.

'Live service' area
An area where universal credit can only be claimed by a person who meets specific 'gateway' conditions.

Main carer
The person in a couple who spends the most time looking after the children, jointly nominated by the couple. The law refers to the 'responsible carer'.

Managed migration
The term used by the Department for Work and Pensions for the process of transferring claimants to universal credit.

Mandatory reconsideration
The requirement to have a decision looked at again by the Department for Work and Pensions before an appeal can be made.

Maximum universal credit
The amount of universal credit that someone is eligible for, before income is taken into account.

Means-tested benefit
A benefit that is only paid if someone's income and capital are low enough.

Minimum income floor
The amount of income a self-employed person is assumed to have, calculated by multiplying the national minimum wage by the number of hours s/he is expected to look for work.

National minimum wage
A set minimum hourly rate that employers must pay.

No recourse to public funds

A restriction that applies to some people subject to immigration control as part of their entry conditions to the UK, prohibiting them from claiming most benefits and tax credits, including universal credit.

Non-consensual conception

Conception that results from an act to which the woman did not agree by choice, or did not have the freedom or capacity to agree by choice.

Non-contributory benefit

A benefit for which entitlement does not depend on having paid a certain amount of national insurance contributions.

Non-dependant

An adult, other than a partner, who lives with the person claiming benefit – eg, a grown-up daughter or son.

Non-means-tested benefit

A benefit that is paid regardless of the amount of someone's income or capital.

Overpayment

An amount of benefit that is paid which is more than a person's entitlement.

Passporting

A term used to describe when entitlement to a particular benefit allows access to other benefits or sources of help.

Penalty as an alternative to prosecution

A type of fine that can be offered to someone instead of being prosecuted, if the Department for Work and Pensions thinks an offence may have been committed.

Person subject to immigration control

Someone who requires leave to enter or remain in the UK but does not have it, or who has leave to remain but is prohibited from having recourse to public funds, or has leave to remain in the UK on the basis of a sponsorship agreement.

Qualifying age for pension credit
Linked to women's pension age, which is currently increasing from age 60, will equalise with men's pension age in 2018 and will reach 67 by 2028.

Real-time information
A system where employers send HM Revenue and Customs information about employees' earnings every time they are paid, which is then used by the Department for Work and Pensions to adjust universal credit awards.

Revision
A statutory method that allows benefit decisions to be changed.

Right to reside
A social security test, mainly affecting European Economic Area nationals, which must be satisfied in order to claim certain benefits.

Sanction
A reduction in a person's universal credit award for failing to meet her/his work-related requirements without a good reason. The term is also used if her/his universal credit is stopped for a set length of time because s/he has committed an offence.

Severely disabled person
Used in the regulations to describe someone getting a higher rate of certain disability benefits.

Short-term advance
An advance of universal credit which can be paid if someone is in hardship while waiting for her/his first payment, if there is a delay in deciding someone's claim and in some other situations.

Sign on
The requirement to attend a jobcentre and sign a declaration at a specified time in order to receive benefit.

Standard allowance
The basic amount of universal credit paid for a single adult or a couple.

Supersession

A statutory method which allows benefit decisions to be changed, usually as a result of a change in circumstances.

Taper

The rate at which a person's maximum universal credit will reduce as her/his earnings increase.

Transitional protection

A way of making sure that a person being transferred to universal credit from another benefit will not receive less money on universal credit than s/he did before.

'Two-child limit'

A restriction of the number of child elements included in an award to a maximum of two. Exceptions apply – eg, where a child is adopted or is part of a multiple birth.

Universal Jobmatch

A government website comprising a database of employment opportunities for use by benefit claimants and work coaches.

Waiting days

Seven days at the start of a universal credit claim when there is usually no entitlement to benefit.

Waiting period

The time at the start of a benefit claim before payment, or payment of certain elements, can start.

Work allowance

The amount of earnings ignored when calculating how much a person's universal credit award is reduced by. The amount depends on personal circumstances.

Work availability

One of the work-related requirements, which means being willing and able to take up paid work, usually immediately and within 90 minutes' travel time of home.

Work coach
Someone employed by the Department for Work and Pensions to draw up claimant commitments, update them and check that claimants are meeting their work-related requirements.

Work-focused interview
One of the work-related requirements, which means attending an interview to discuss future work opportunities and the barriers to work.

Work preparation
One of the work-related requirements, which includes carrying out activities to prepare for a future return to work, such as increasing skills or doing a work placement.

Work-related requirements
The activities that a person must undertake to continue to receive the full amount of universal credit.

Work search
One of the work-related requirements, which means normally spending 35 hours a week looking for work.

Index